THE BEA[illegible]
DIFFERENT DRUMS

THE BEAT OF DIFFERENT DRUMS

How I left behind glam rock and went on a journey of many lifetimes

JOHN RICHARDSON

'Jayadev'

FITZROVIA PRESS

published by Fitzrovia Press 2011

Fitzrovia Press
10 Grafton Mews, London W1T 5JG
www.fitzroviapress.co.uk

Printed and bound in Great Britain by
Good News Digital Books, Essex
set in Sabon 10.5 pt
on 90gsm Bookwove FSC certified paper

ISBN 978-0-9561846-5-8

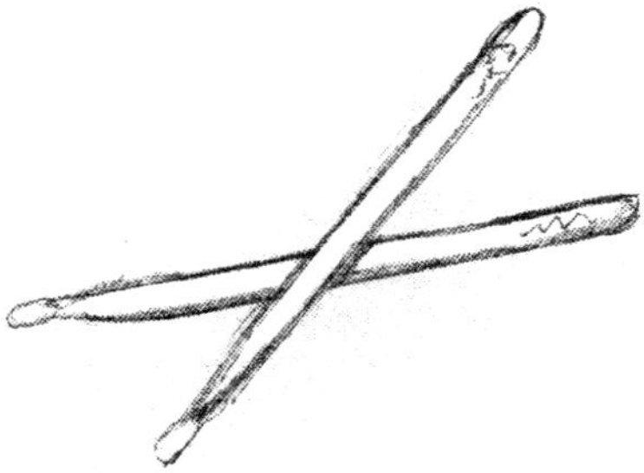

JOHN RICHARDSON was born and raised in Essex. He achieved success and fame in his early twenties as founder member, drummer and vocalist for seventies Glam Rock band the Rubettes, penning many of their hits. In 1983 he left the Rubettes to concentrate on a career in alternative medicine and past-life therapy. He received instruction in the spiritual wisdom of Krishna, and was given the name Jayadev. In recent years he has developed his own brand of music and mantra therapy, releasing several New Age recordings as a solo artist with New World Music. Jayadev now tours with the re-formed Rubettes and teaches mantra yoga. He doesn't have much time for hobbies these days but when he gets a moment he likes to sleep.

Contents

Preface

THIS PREFACE SHOULD READ, 'This is my story.' But to be honest I was a famous Rubette for fifteen minutes. Many musicians drummed better, sang better, sold more records and looked better than me. However, in our brief mayfly existence, we sold records in millions of units (nearly twice a baker's dozen). Then, after experiencing virtually everything I'd ever dreamed of, I went on an inner journey and experienced things beyond my wildest dreams.

Rags to riches to rags is not an uncommon experience in the music industry. She has a canny knack of sucking you in and blowing you out without too much compunction. So I never took it too personally. In fact, I'm grateful for what destiny did to me. Sitting right there, between the confusion wrought by her mighty inhalations and exhalations, I found myself and all the riches I could ever handle.

Please forgive the occasional expletive. I didn't think you'd mind the *&*%$ stuff – it has helped me tell it like it really was.

John Richardson
March 2010

Words from Boy George

As transformations go few can be more unlikely than the one made by John Richardson. He has been many things over many lifetimes it seems, but how do you go from being a flared-trouser wearing drummer for 70s pop combo the Rubettes to saffron-robed spiritual healer and Krishna devotee?

Like most of my generation I first knew of John, now Jayadev, when he was part of the Rubettes back in the 70s. I bought those quirky records and sang along to the doo-wop melodies, never once imagining that one day we would be friends, or that I would receive some of his legendary healing!

It was after my first trip to India in 1990 that I met John. I was recording a new song, *Bow Down Mister,* which I wrote written on my travels around India. My producer Bruce Forrest announced in his brash American drawl, 'We need some proper devotees on this track. Know any serious Krishna dudes?'

The only one I knew was Nayana Biram with whom I had just spent three weeks in India. As far as I knew he wasn't much of a singer but I did know of a Hare Krishna temple in Soho and decided to make a phone call to see if I could rustle up some serious Krishna dudes!

I'll never forget that phone call. The following afternoon a bunch of devotees in full regalia arrived at the recording studio and I nervously played them the song, worrying that I might offend them in some way. Far from being offended they bowed down in front of me, which made me blush. John (Jayadev) was carrying a large drum. He told me I would be blessed by Krishna and said something about Lord Krishna pulling me up to heaven! It was all very overwhelming, but I was excited because I knew I was about to get one hell of a joyous vocal session. Bruce Forrest had also hired a gospel choir, who eyed the devotees suspiciously as the engineer arranged microphones so that we could capture the heavenly voices of our two choirs singing to their different Gods. One exotic and beautifully blue, the other white and serene with the hair of a lamb! It was a crazy session but Bruce's idea to call in a gospel choir and get some 'serious Krishna dudes' was inspired and life-changing for me.

From the moment I laid eyes on Jayadev I was convinced we had met before and when he told me he had once been a Rubette I nearly fell of my metaphorical platform boots! The recording of *Bow Down Mister* was most definitely a spiritual experience and I believe the song has a touch of magic.

When *Bow Down Mister* was released it didn't exactly set the world on fire until something strange happened in Germany. I had almost given up on the song when I received a phone call from my manager Tony Gordon to say that Virgin Records in Germany wanted me to fly in for three days to do promotion for the single. I thought it was weird because it was months after the official release of the single and as far as I was concerned the song was a ceremonious flop!

A small local radio station had been playing Bow Down Mister on heavy rotation. They received a complaint from the state church who felt they should not be promoting a cult like the Hare Krishnas. The story appeared in the German press and almost overnight loads of other radio stations started playing it in defiance of the church. Suddenly, *Bow Down Mister* stormed to the top of the German pop charts and I spent the next year or so performing it on TV and in concert all over Europe. In each country I was joined by local 'serious Krishna dudes' and together we chanted the name of Lord Krishna. During that period I also performed with Jayadev to about thirty thousand devotees in Moscow. It was a seriously amazing time in my life!

I have known Jayadev and his lovely family for the best part of twenty years and I feel blessed to have him in my life. I don't mean to blow smoke up his dhoti but I have to say that he is truly spiritual in every sense of the word. I joke that he has a Ready Brek glow around him. When he walks into a room he brings calm and you can't help thinking 'whatever he's on, I'll have some of that!'

It's hard to connect him to the bloke in the wide-lapelled jacket and flared trousers from that quirky 70s pop group, or imagine him battling with French coppers, worrying about his nobbly nose or pulling a fast one on Arnold Schwarzenegger. *Different Drums* documents John's early days as a struggling musician, the rise of the Rubettes and his discovery of Krishna Consciousness. It's a choice read for any musician who wants to know about life before 'boil in a bag fame' when musicians actually had to put in some hard graft to build a career.

As a rule, spiritual conversion tends to make Jack a very dull boy, but Jayadev is still the same engaging, good-natured cheeky chap he ever was. His story is full of laugh-out-loud anecdotes written with great affection and good humour. These days he's back drumming for the Rubettes, which adds another twist to his exceptional tale. It proves that if you have enough 'Krishna Baby Love' you can have it all!

Hare Krishna,

Boy George xx

Foreword by Dave Bartram

TOURING IN A ROCK 'N' ROLL BAND can be an arduous business. Hours of travelling, day and night, flee-bitten beds in damp, noisy hotel rooms, whiling away what seem like light years in spartan dressing rooms waiting for the sound-checks to end and the theatre doors to open. These are experiences that all stalwarts of the gigging industry become hardened to!

Over the past twenty-five years or so, my band Showaddywaddy have toured with the Rubettes (the 'Barbs we nicknamed them – as in Ru-barb) both in the UK and Europe on numerous occasions, and it has been my good fortune to have become a close friend of John Richardson.

To have someone like John on the road is a true blessing. He simply thrives on making life better for those around him. Aching muscles, strained vocal chords, tired bodies and fractious minds: John has a gift of being giving comfort to all of these. Either with his healing hands or mental strength he possesses an uncanny ability to not only alter one's mindset, but to inspire and remove any negativity almost instantly. I remember one particular occasion when I was suffering from a chest complaint, and arrived at the next tour date to be greeted by a weird aroma from the backstage kitchen and saw John emerge from a cloud of steam. He'd stopped en-route to gather nettles, herbs and other forest remedies to make a rare and precious brew that left a horrible mess inside the in-house kettle. However, I have to say the effects of John's potion were strangely efficacious!

John is himself a rare and precious human being, and I am privileged to be asked to add these words as a prelude to the incredible story of a remarkable man. After all, anyone who's called the current Governor of California a rather common expletive bears a voice that needs to be heard by all.

Dave Bartram
May 2010

Acknowledgements

I WANT TO THANK the following well wishers and friends who have played some large or small part in the appearance of this book

Firstly, the King of Puri who insisted I record the tales within for posterity. For Julie Spearritt for the first encouraging edits. Kripamoya Prabhu who read it over the Christmas holiday 'without putting it down.' Bryce Little for printing out the many manuscripts for the vital labour of constructive criticisms. Boy George for readily and lovingly offering his foreword. Dave Bartram for his enlivening preface.

Ranchor Prime for his love and appreciation of my work. His beloved daughter Anasuya Prime for the final edits.

Kate Tucker Vincent for her assistance with the chapter on Cambridge. Mark Hayley for his dating and timing of Rubettes hits.

The Rubettes themselves for tolerating both my material and spiritual madness.

My sweet Lord for bringing about a cessation of the suffering of the beginning and middle periods of my life by gifting me with a sweet end.

May you all who read this obtain something that will grow corn in your own lives – and if you already have some grown may this year's be a bumper harvest!

May I thank from the bottom of my heart all those who

filled my mind and heart with joy and wonder with the revelations hidden in theirs, especially Wofgang Mozart.

In some cases, to preserve people's privacy, I have changed their names.

And finally, my dear family of Saci, Gaurangi and Siddhartha for teaching and showing me so much.

Love,

Jayadev

Part One

Dreams of Drumming

Rubettes

Prologue

LATE 1974. SIRENS.

Our two big black cars, a Rolls-Royce and a Daimler limousine, park hurriedly on the hard shoulder of an autoroute west of Paris, and seven long-haired incredulous occupants are forced out of the vehicles, hands ordered high into the air.

Unable to comprehend what is taking place, we stand dazed and shivering on a grassy knoll as ashen-faced gendarmes swarm around us and the French rain gives us a thorough lashing.

Parked behind the Rolls and Daimler are two meat wagons (that's police vans to you). A sharp prod from the gendarme. The cold nozzle of his gun in my back.

Next to me is Alan Williams, lead singer, famous for his high-pitched voice. Alan knows a little French and manages to make himself heard above the din.

'Do you know who we effin' well are?' he screams in his best French, only to be summarily ignored by our Gallic tormentors.

Tony Thorpe, our guitarist and the educated one amongst us, stays cool. Realising the police are intent on frisking us and that none of them understand English, Mick Clarke, our bass player and the driest comedian amongst us, mimics a WW2 pilot.

'I say, Wing Co!' he calls over to me, 'Would you kindly

drop Dorothy a line and tell her I died bravely?'

'May the good Lord bless you, Carruthers,' I reply in my best English Wing Commander's accent. 'God, I wish I was going with you.'

Pete, our humourless keyboardist, spoils the tone, shouting, 'Fuck off, you fascist pigs!'

Roy, our twenty-four stone, chain-smoking manager, asks permission for a final cigarette and puts it between his lips, where it dangles defiantly, unlit.

Poor Tony, our guitarist and the least confrontational among us, is being jostled and threatened by the gendarmes. They wrongly suspect him as being the driver of the car due to his sitting in the front passenger seat which of course is the driver's position in France.

'You driver! You driver!' they scream whilst Fat Roy, the real driver, starts to laugh, realising our little mild-mannered Tony is being targeted as the villain, though we still have no idea what for.

Alan manages to calm things by putting together a few understandable words.

'Sugar Baby Love?' he asks hopefully. I sense a breakthrough in communications when one of the gendarmes raises an eyebrow. *Sugar Baby Love* is the name of the Rubettes' first big French hit.

'Tonight!' I blurt out. This is our second big hit. Again, there is some semblance of recognition.

Slowly their expressions soften and realisation dawns upon our captors that they have arrested the biggest British pop group in French musical history. Perhaps it's not every day that these gendarmes take the Rubettes, Glam Rock idols, in for questioning. It doesn't mean we are free to go though.

Alan, the most easily recognizable among us, is offered a seat with the commander in the front seat of the meat wagon, while the rest of us are squeezed in the back with two gendarmes, now looking decidedly more relaxed.

Convinced that music is the international language, we start to sing some of our hits to pass the time, strumming air guitars and tapping on soaking-wet trousered knees until we arrive at the French version of the 'nick' not far from the autoroute.

Alan is ushered into the Commander's office while the rest of us wait in reception. No longer fearing for our lives, we soon tire of entertaining our captors and chat among ourselves, telling anti-French jokes about our undeserved and untimely arrest. The whole episode now seems rather amusing and one for the memoirs that John, the drummer, will exaggerate the hell out of thirty years later.

Tony, now somewhat placated, suggests our arrest may have been due to the offensive lyrics of our latest French release, *Allez Oop*. Bad taste is hardly a crime, though, so we burst into song again.

'Allez allez allez oop, you're my cuppa tea, my bowl of soup.'

Actually we deserve to be arrested for that, but it's what we always do in France – we take the mick. Us English have been doing it to the French since as far back as the humiliating Norman Conquest.

Polydor, our record label at the time, had offices in every major country of the world. It was normal that if one of your artists had a hit in England, that same recording would be released in other Polydor territories. So it was that in country after country our single was released to great acclaim and success. All, that is, except France. They refused to release it there, and it remained unheard on French soil.

Why, you might ask, would it not be successful there?

There was one good reason. The French wanted to keep out the foreign invaders. They did that by keeping their crafty eyes on the world charts. When they saw a big new hit they would swiftly embargo it and a French artist would quickly do a cover version, so keeping the whole thing, as far as possible, in house. That was why the French had their own Elvis, their own Frank Sinatra, and so on.

So the Frenchies nicked our hit.

One day, weeks after we had become number one practically everywhere else, our recording manager, Andy Stephens, came rushing into Polydor's demo studio in Stratford Place, off Oxford Street in London.

'The dirty rotten bastards!' he exclaimed in an agitated voice. 'Those crafty sods have put out *Sugar Baby Love* on another record label, and some guy called Dave is singing it!'

He paused for a second as we absorbed the initial impact, with echoes of 'Bastard!' and other spicier expletives. Then came the cruellest words we could hear.

'It's number one! Look!' And he showed us an article in Music Week with a picture of a happy, grinning Dave, the French singer. Six sets of eyes turned green with envy.

'Bastard!' everyone roared again in unison, making Stephanie the receptionist spill our tray of hot tea. What compounded the theft was the picture of Dave wearing exactly the same outfit as the Rubettes had become famous for: white suit, white cap, and black and white brogues. Not only had Dave nicked our record, he'd nicked our identity too.

'Bastard, effin bastard!' echoed round the studio.

Soon afterwards, our music director had a terse conversation with his French counterpart. To cut a long story short, Polydor France reluctantly agreed to release the Rubettes original version of *Sugar Baby Love.*

Soon we were booked to appear on France's biggest musical variety show, hosted by the infamous Guy Lux, known for his egotistical tantrums. We innocently set about our job of attempting what hardly any other British act had done up to that time – to conquer La France.

Our rehearsal started around ten in the morning. They routined us with the customary camera shots and lighting paraphernalia, while Guy Lux stood there bellowing orders in French, completely ignoring us. It was as if we didn't exist. Then we were sent to our cupboard of a dressing room to wait indefinitely. Time passed. We were offered nothing to eat or drink. I knew we shouldn't complain, because we didn't want to lose the golden opportunity of succeeding in France, the fourth biggest record-buying nation in the world.

Finally, after an eight-hour wait, we were called for the dress rehearsal. The audience were present and we felt an expectant buzz as we delivered *Sugar Baby Love*. Alan turned on his smouldering presentation. My part, where I stood up at my drum kit and spoke a few tongue-in-cheek lines, seemed to captivate the audience, if I do say so myself. After the dress rehearsal, people were bursting through security to touch us or autograph-hunt as we tried to get back to our cupboard.

Shortly afterwards a representative of Guy Lux came with some unexpected news.

'Guy Lux says you must go,' he proclaimed in a barely-decipherable accent.

'You mean go back to the stage for another rehearsal?' asked Alan.

'Non! You go back to L'Angleterre!'

'Whaaaaaat! Who the fuck does he…'

We had no choice but to leave, persona non TV show. We never did find out why we were thrown off the show, but before we went, Roy Farrant, our manager, stampeded into the audience like a wild elephant.

'Rubettes are out! Rubettes are gone!' he bellowed, and it only took one person in the audience to understand the English and translate for the rest before the outrage and injustice became clear. We were later told there was a riot.

At Charles De Gaulle Airport, severely pissed off, we were

about to board our plane home when a messenger appeared with astonishing news. We were wanted back on the show. Lux had recanted.

After the customary 'We don't care', 'We're going home', 'Who does he think he is?' the idea of relieving the producers of a few of their hard earned francs overcame all other considerations and we jubilantly rushed back to the studio.

Guy Lux never apologised or gave a reason for his behaviour. We burst onto the podium in our dapper whites with matching caps and the audience erupted into ecstatic applause. It was almost as satisfying as seeing our record at number one two weeks later. French sales of *Sugar Baby Love* came to around one-and-a-half million.

France was an enigma. The ordinary people embraced us with open hearts and were some of the warmest individuals you could hope to meet, but in the entertainment industry we met some of the most arrogant individuals you are ever likely to cross a croissant with. This caused us so much frustration that we never wanted to speak or hear the French language again. Although we went to France many times since, doing TV, radio and gigs, I swore never to learn the language and I never have.

Which brings me back to the gendarmes by the autoroute. I was wishing I'd never made that vow. I would've given anything to know what was going on. What had we done to deserve this?

The answer soon came. Alan strolled out of the commander's office with a huge smile. In his hands were some publicity photos he always carried with him.

'Sign these lads. Everything's sorted.'

Alan explained that all this stemmed from an earlier incident on the autoroute between Mickey and a mad French motorist.

We'd been travelling in convoy toward the Chateau recording studio in western Paris, when a motorist flew past our Daimler and overtook Mickey, who was driving his Rolls a short distance ahead. This insane motorist got directly in front of Mickey's car and slammed on his brakes. We were all thrown forward as the cars came to an abrupt halt. All this happened in the fast lane of a rain-soaked and misty motorway.

The usual expletives poured forth because we had needlessly come so close to death. The French motorist and his unfortunate family sped off again, with Mickey in hot pursuit. We tailed the two cars mainly to see what our normally mild-mannered bassist would do next. To our amazement, at eighty miles an hour, Mickey overtook the speeding driver and slowed to halt, leaving our three cars once again stopped on the fast lane.

Mickey jumped out, swearing at the guy, but somehow the Frenchman pulled out from between us and drove off into the mist. He then apparently told the police we were a bunch of villains from England who had threatened the lives of him and his family.

My reason for opening with this anecdote is not so much the story itself, but because of a special significance it had for me.

Prior to the France trip, I had twice dreamt that we were being held on the side of a road by men with machine guns. I told the lads at the time, because I always felt my dreams were significant. I thought this one might be a symbolic foretelling of the break-up of the band. At the time they all just laughed at me. But halfway through our autoroute adventure, when Tony was wet and scared, surrounded by machine gun-wielding police, he suddenly remembered.

'Fuck me, John! You told us this would happen!'

All through my life, at crucial moments, such premonitions

have mysteriously appeared in my consciousness. Little did I know that I was to spend most of my life dedicated to understanding this guidance and giving it to others.

One

WHEN I WAS FOURTEEN I had a dream which foretold my future. I was playing a set of white drums, doing triplets, paradiddles, semi quavers, all kinds of things that I had no knowledge of at the time. In waking life I was completely unable to perform such exacting tasks. It was wonderful and when I woke up I knew what I wanted to do with my life. I would be a musician; a drummer.

My determination to play drums was also fired by a little envy. Mickey Paine, the boy living in the prefab across the road, had a snare drum which he thumped for an annoying couple of hours every day. My inflated teenage ego couldn't let Mickey, my arch rival, get ahead of me.

But how would I get a drum kit? Not just a snare, but a full-blown kit with cymbals and pedals?

Only one thing to do: work and save.

I already had a paper round. I'd been doing it since I was twelve, working for Mrs Hall's newsagents in Ockendon. Whenever I could, I also worked a milk round.

It took a year to save up enough because I always gave too much change to my customers. Many times I was short and actually owed Mrs Hall money after a week's hard work.

How I dreaded those Saturday morning count-ups in the village shop. Derek, Mrs Hall's son, would get down the takings book and add up the amount I should have in my weather-beaten leather bag – pennies, halfpennies and farthings in the front, silver and notes in the back. I waited, expecting the total would be less than it should be. I can still hear his voice.

'You're short!'

The first time he said it, I thought he was referring to my size. If he says anything about my nose, I thought, I'm going to chuck the job in and tell him where to stick his paper round. But he didn't and, after a year of working and saving, I climbed triumphantly aboard the red 370 bus to Romford on my quest to find the nearest music store.

It was my longest trip alone till then, about seven miles, made even longer by my yearning to see a real drum kit.

There, in the front window of the Romford's Pioneer music shop on the corner of South Street, was the very same drum kit I had played in my dream. It was beautiful and it was white.

So began my music career. The focus of my very existence from that day onwards was my Olympic drum kit.

I even began to forget about my nose.

I used to have a cute, small, turned-up nose, but at the onset of puberty, I swear, I woke up one morning to see with horror that overnight it had tripled in size. I asked my mum for some cooking oil to rub into my nose every evening and I'd squeeze, pinch and flatten it to try to make it seem smaller. Worse, when passing a pretty girl I had to sniff deeply so as to draw my nostrils in and reduce its size, hoping to increase my chances of being adored, or at least not deplored, by the opposite sex.

Years later, a girl from my class revealed that all the girls had noticed this funny breathing noise coming from me as I passed them on the crowded pavement when school finished. Thinking I had some strange disorder or twitch, she claimed, had put off quite a number of her friends, including herself, from wanting to go out with me.

My family, made up of my parents, Doreen and Charlie, my three brothers, Charlie, Peter and Ian, and myself, lived on a housing estate of prefabs built in the Essex countryside by German prisoners of war. They were tiny two-bedroomed concrete bungalows thrown up in a hurry to re-house people from bombed-out parts of East London. Mum and Dad had one room and we brothers in bunk-beds had t'other. Due to the wafer-thin walls you could hear the people living four houses away when they argued. And now an Olympic drum kit also resounded through the estate. I squeezed in an hour's practice every day as soon as I returned from school and before Dad came home from work. The din was like a tumult from hell but fortunately my poor mum and the neighbours never complained.

After a short while I got permission to use the treasured radiogram, the Richardson's only luxury, and turning the volume to full pelt I played along to Gerry and the Pacemakers *I Like It* and Mike Berry's *Don't Ya Think It's Time*. It was ecstatic, just like being in my own group.

Funnily just last year the Rubettes played on the same bill as both Mike Berry and Gerry Marsden, now nearly in their seventies. People call him Gerry and his Pacemaker.

Before too long I was way ahead of Mickey's boring tap-tap-tap bosh-bosh-bosh. Mickey's dad, Roger, was in the throes of a mental breakdown. I used to see him standing, drably dressed and in his slippers, at the front door of his house, tapping his foot to the beat of military marches blaring from the wireless inside the house. I learned to hate that type of music. It was like a rhythmic harbinger of death on the battlefield. To this day, if I hear a military march all I see is Roger Payne's tortured face as he stood by his front door.

One day Roger took an overdose of antidepressants and tragically choked to death on his own vomit. Fortunately,

Mickey and his brother Raymond didn't see it happen. Their mother Audrey did though. Dad offered our home to the boys that first night, so that Audrey could compose herself. Mickey lay next to me in my bunk bed and Raymond lay weeping next to my elder brother Charlie in the upper bunk.

Late that night Audrey came into our bedroom and woke her boys with kisses and whispers, and Mickey and Raymond went home with their mum to 49 Celandine Close across the street. I couldn't stand the pain the boys were in and threw myself into my drumming with renewed vigour.

During one ecstatic practice session I remembered the dream I'd had a year earlier, and felt I was playing the exact beats I had seen and heard before.

My own first experience of life's tragedy was a more pathetic affair. I spent several halcyon years in Benyon Infants and Junior School, where I adored my beloved teacher Miss Cox. For two heady, love-filled years I worshipped everything about her, from her floral print dresses to her swept-back auburn hair and her wonderful voice teaching us Jack and Jill nursery rhymes.

Then one dark and calamitous day we were told by our headmistress that my darling Miss Cox was shortly to be leaving our school to teach at another far away. I cried uncontrollably throughout her last afternoon's class, attributing the tears to a stomach ache rather than heartache. After school Miss Cox kindly allowed me to accompany her to the bus stop, where the red 370 bus would cruelly carry her away forever.

Seeing my torment, she took me to Mrs Pook's sweetshop, on the corner of West Road and Ockendon High Street, and bought me a Kit Kat. It was an act of love that has probably never been equalled in my life. It lasted for months under my pillow, where night after night I would hold it to my cheek, pray to it and try to feel her presence once again, as tears ran in rivulets onto my pillow. Miss Cox, where are yoooooou?

One night I carelessly left that chocolate keepsake on my pillow, silently crying myself to sleep. The said bar must have fallen to the bedroom floor because in the morning Charlie was gone from his bed, the Kit Kat had gone and Miss Cox's presence was cruelly torn from my life.

Cousin Barry lived in the same street as me, number 12 Celandine Close, and I lived at number 35. Barry and I notched up a number of successful scrumping missions in Mrs Scott's orchard, and were getting a little smug that we were never caught. One sunny day we swaggered through the pear, apple and plum orchard without hiding or crouching, taking any fruit we fancied. This particular day we were showing little Willy Frost and my younger brother Pete how big grown-up eleven-year-olds like us ruled the kingdom of Mrs Scott's orchard. With our arms full of fruity booty, we walked proudly back to our disciples who were hidden behind the bushes by the ditch. Miraculously, Mrs Scott jumped out from behind the walnut tree, barring our escape. I say miraculously because she was in her nineties. We nearly died, caught red-handed in full view of our adoring followers by the formidable Mrs Scott. We were dumbstruck and near to tears as she angrily questioned us.

'I know who you are, so now I'm going to come round to your houses tonight and tell your parents what you've done.'

I froze with terror. My dad was straight – he wouldn't have a button in the house if it had been stolen. What to do?

'What's your name and address, laddie?' she snapped, looking at Barry first.

Barry was bricking it as badly as I was, but in that fraction of a second he came up with an ingenious idea.

'My name is John Richardson and I live at 35 Celandine

Road,' he replied craftily.

Wow! Barry had given my name and address, what a good idea. She'll never get him now.

'And you,' she said, looking menacingly at me. 'Who are you and where do you live?'

Picking up Barry's lead, I gave my answer.

'Barry Richardson, 12 Celandine Rd.'

'Mark my words, I'll be round tonight to tell your parents what you two have been up to.'

We feigned fear and shame, I bringing my hands to my gasping mouth, and Barry wringing his in despair, but as soon as we were released and jumped across the ditch to head home we began laughing derisively, certain we had got clean away.

That night, Mrs Scott stunned us by turning up at the right addresses and spilling the shameful beans. Our outraged fathers duly gave us a 'good clipping round the ear'ole,' as it was referred to at the time. As a young lad I can remember how his hands seemed like spades when he gave me a deserved clump. Funny, they seemed even bigger and harder when (at least in my reckoning) he hit me for no good reason.

Bigger than Dad's hand was the brute hand of destiny that flung me in the direction of Lennard Secondary Modern School, alias Stalag 39. There the older boys subjected the new kids to hell. They thrust my innocent head down the grimy toilet bowl as a first day welcome. You had to live in fear until that sweet day arrived when we discovered the guts or strength to punch the snot out of them. I was no wimp, and pretty soon us new boys learned to bully, cajole and intimidate the weaker students. I hated doing it, but we had to maintain the profile or we would be dead meat.

We had a groundsman called Bob, an affable character popular with the boys. We used to flock to his little garden shed at the side of the playground at break time and chit-chat with him. We also hoped to glimpse some of the saucy pictures that adorned the creosote-soaked walls of his hut. Sometimes he let us have a drag on a roll-up which he deftly created with his muddy fingers from a tin box marked Golden Virginia, faded from years of dedicated service to Bob's habit.

Bob put bets on the horses for us. I never had any money of course, but I seemed to know the winners of the big races. My friend, Keith Neil, wore the latest clothes and always had cash for a bet. I remember sitting at my desk directly behind Keith in geography class. I would hear him whisper.

'John? Is it going to be Loppy Lugs for the 2.30 at Aintree today?' He would pass the racing page from the daily paper under my desk, and I would run my finger down the list of names until I stopped at the eventual winner.

Maybe this psychic stuff ran in the family. My father often knew when family members who lived miles away were pregnant or ill. He used to have dreams in which he got the date a baby was born and other details. We had no phone in those days, but he would say to mum, 'Your sister had a baby girl this morning, x pounds, x ounces.' He was rarely wrong. Pity it didn't work for him on the horses, which he gambled on almost daily to try to improve our impoverished lot.

Mickey Sangster was the neighbourhood's best sportsman, though I reckon it was his close proximity to the Field that gave him an unfair advantage. His house was in the alley right next to the oval-shaped patch of grass we (ingeniously) called the Field. He could jump out of bed, over the wire fence and into its long grass in one bound.

A giant elm tree stood proudly in the centre. That trusty tree was a true friend to me, always ready to facilitate a hurried climb when my older brother Charlie was after my blood, always ready to deliver my rebounds if there was no one else to play football with, and wide enough for a wicket if you painted the stumps on its trunk.

I should have been a better sportsman than I was, but when I got all dressed up in my football kit to steal a march on the others, I would get distracted by the magnificence of the spreading elm. Hiding my old leather ball in the tall grass, I would clamber forty feet up and sit there singing Lonnie Donegan songs. When other kids arrived to play, I would clamber down, rub my knees in the mud to prove to my dad (our coach) that I'd been practising, then grab my half-deflated ball and run home, with less footballing skills than I started with.

Our great summer Olympics were held each August in the school holidays. Almost every neighbourhood kid participated. The prizes came from our bank of old comics, books and magazines that we kept at Mickey's house. Some of us dreamed of standing on the orange box podium, the cheers of the vanquished ringing in our ears, but I dreamed of spending my time in the company of Roy of the Rovers, Biffo the Bear and Mickey Mouse. Most kids had a comic delivered to their home each week. I knew who they were and what they read, because I delivered my friends' comics. While they were still curled up in their warm beds, I would be blissfully dragging the comics off the early morning train from London, pulling them on a wheelbarrow up the hill to Mrs Hall's, folding them neatly for Mrs Hall to compile the delivery numbers and finally delivering them. My working morning started at 4am and finished at 8am. Then a hot bowl of Scot's porridge oats and a four mile run to school. I was seriously fit but quite unaware of it, until an older boy hit me in the goollies with a billiard cue. In an unconscious reflex I laid him flat.

Mostly dear old mum and dad didn't have money for school dinners, so I had to return home at lunchtime for more porridge or potato sarnies, or sometimes sugar ones – delish!

Despite tight finances I used to get the Beano, my brother Charlie got the Dandy, and then we shared the Eagle, which featured the marvellous Dan Dare and the irksome Mekon. Oh how we looked forward to devouring Dennis the Menace cartoons and Desperate Dan stories in our bunk beds.

Unfortunately, our constant fighting made Mum's life hell. When we finished reading our own comics, we were both desperate to read the other's, but too proud to admit it. I overcame this by reading other boys' Dandy comics, page by page as I delivered them to each house. Because of this, my round took me an hour and a half instead of an hour. I read other comics too, until the time taken to do my deliveries stretched to nearly two hours, and I was late for school on comic delivery days. Added to this, customers at the end of the round got irate due to later and later deliveries, and complained to Mrs Hall that they had to go to work without their paper.

For me, our neighbourhood summer Olympics were the answer. Each contestant put his comics into the prize pool at the kids' bank. If I could win enough races or throw the javelins (broom poles) far enough, I could have all the comics a boy ever dreamed of.

Everyone competed in everything. Juniors vied for supremacy against seniors in the hundred yards sprint, hoping for a hidden pothole to annihilate the enemy. High jumpers would execute the scissor jump with great dexterity until the bar (chicken wire borrowed from Alfie Biscoe's shed) was lifted above the three foot mark. That was the point that separated the men from the boys.

This particular year, Mickey Paine was the favourite to carry off the high jump title and didn't come in until a massive four feet was reached. His first jump cleared it with plenty to spare. I was kissing goodbye to at least six comics when Mickey landed badly and broke his wrist.

I stoically maintained to the adjudicator Mickey Sangster

that I was intending to jump when four foot three was reached, and seeing that I was the only other competitor that year I was declared the dubious winner.

But wait. Who's this? We gasped in disgust. A girl? A blinkin' girl wants to try?

Irene English lined up to take the jump. Until then it was a boys only event, and then here came this girl trying to lower the tone of the whole games.

I tried to put her off.

'What comic did you put in to Mickey's bank?' I asked derisively.

'Bunty.'

At this we magnificent boys roared with laughter. Bunty indeed! No self-respecting boy would be seen within a javelin's throw of that.

After the derision had subsided, Irene drew a deep breath and launched her long lanky legs at the bar.

She soared over it just like Mickey. Her friend Lyn Green, standing to one side, the only other female there, provided the shrieking victorious voice that threatened to smash our notion of male supremacy to smithereens, spoiling our summer Olympics forever.

We set the bar at four foot three.

Flushed with success, Irene lifted her skirt, unconsciously showing off her not-unattractive freckled limbs, and flew through the air. Fear of humiliating defeat at the hands of a girl threw the whole picture into slow motion in my head. All I remember is the robust scissoring of her legs as she prepared to sail over the bar. I winked to Mickey Sangster at one end of the string to lift it an inch or two, but he was in love with her from the moment he detected those long freckled legs. Pie-eyed for Irene, Mickey ignored my remonstrations.

Then it happened. Call me naive if you want, but I never knew it could, not this, not in the female species, but it did –

the most shocking life-altering gift from the gods. Irene was about to clear the bar, her lissom limbs stretched akimbo, when...

PARP!

She farted.

Wind assisted, she cleared the bar and every nasty little boy, desperate to regain the immoral high ground, exaggeratedly bellowed with laughter. Irene and Lyn scuttled away from that male-dominated arena, never to return.

I was gutted. Even though I was the winner by default, Mickey Sangster, the tournament's adjudicator, insisted that if I wanted my six-comic prize, I had to take Irene's Bunty. Oh, the shame of it.

Next came the pole vault. We cut branches from trees where later the Ford Motor Company built their factory, and skinned off the bumps and twigs to make our poles. I shone in that competition, and won Film Fun as a treasured prize.

I was good at throwing too, spending season after season practicing with unripe fruits on our enemies from Tamarisk Road when they came near any of our hideouts. Our hideouts were holes dug in the ground, covered with corrugated iron from old Anderson shelters, then hidden beneath grass and dirt. My dugout took me six hard weeks of sweat and toil to make.

The nearby sandpits were a haven for practising stone skimming. On the steep hills leading down to the deep water we held mock battles with 40-year old Alfie Biscoe, our neighbour who had suffered a nervous breakdown and was thus unemployed. We re-employed Alfie in the service of our fun-filled sports, as we thought up game after glorious game to while away those summer days.

Once, playing above the sandpits, it was Alfies' turn to drive us boys from the crest of the hill. In true-spirited defence of that sacred position, overcome by the zeal of the moment, one of us pushed Alfie with a stout hob-nailed boot back down the slope toward the water. He skidded hilariously (we thought) on his arse. Unknown to us, broken shards of glass were concealed in the grassy slope. The glass ripped into poor Alfie's ample behind. Afterwards we always referred to that day as Alfie's Arsenic Day.

The summer Olympics culminated in the marathon, which my brother Charlie won every year. Though we seemed to hate each other, I secretly admired his skills as an amazing batsman, goalie and marathon runner. He was the youngest boy ever to score fifty runs in a prestigious inter-district cricket match, and was up for the Donald Bradman award for his feat, until they found out he was too young to have been playing in the first place. No prize for poor old Charlie.

The prize everyone wanted to win, though, was our kid's Olympic marathon. If you came first you could choose any number of comics and you really were the big cheese. And dear old Charlie won, year after frustrating year. Instead of starting at a moderate pace he would sprint out across the Olympic field, heading south down our alley, cross the allotment path, then zoom up the station hill and disappear down the other side, before most of us had even reached the allotments. This tactic broke the spirit of most of the competitors, and some, like me, just gave up then and there. In that year, 1957, consigned to yet another failed marathon attempt, we retired to Alfie's house to lick our wounds.

Alfie, single and in his forties, sensed our dismay.

'Who's up for a ride on the bike?' he said.

Alfie had a silver Triumph Tiger Cub 125. I darted my hand in the air before the others.

'Let's follow Charlie,' I shouted, and in a trice I was hanging onto Alfie's abundant waist as we sped over the hill in the direction of the Marathon Miracle. He was so fast there was as yet no sign of him, just a few straggling stoics determined to at least come in a brave second.

After five minutes of exhilarating curves and tight bends on the farm roads around Ockendon, Pea Lane came in sight. This was where the marathon runners would be turning right. And indeed we caught our first glimpse of the intrepid athlete, Marvellous Charles, turning right, still maintaining formidable speed, due to being perched on the crossbar of Mickey O'Shea's bicycle.

The full penny only dropped later, when we realised that Mickey was never there in previous years when Charlie 'won' his marathons – he always had some excuse. Year after bloody year, there he was, picking Charlie up on the other side of the station bridge, biking him round the six-mile course and dropping him off at Ockendon village, where he would sprint as hard as he could down Main Road, into Lime Road, round Tamarisk Road (just enough to generate a sweat) and triumphantly burst through into the north alleyway that led to the ribbonned finish line. There he theatrically fell to the ground, every bloody year, clutching his cramped stomach, grimacing and rolling in agony from his heroic exertions, amid tumultuous applause from kids and adults.

Around this time puberty slammed her fist into our private parts, causing them and the addled brain loosely connected to them to run wild. Body parts doubled in size while other vital parts refuse to get involved, causing much consternation for the blighted among us in the communal school showers.

No one was prepared for what those invisible hormones had done to the older boys and would likewise do to us. All of a sudden it seemed the little squirt that made you feel secure in the knowledge that there was always gonna be one person you could lick in a fight or give the occasional Chinese burn, had grown a foot taller and you were offering to lick his boots.

From around ten till twelve years I had renounced thoughts of the fairer sex, in favour of stamp collecting, ditch jumping, rabbit breeding and tree diving. Then, in the space of a fortnight, girls suddenly went from something I could take or leave to all I thought about every waking moment of every agitated day. Suddenly girls looked like women, boys looked like men, and the whole world was never to be the same again.

Our Social Skills teacher gave us a special class.

'Soon you will be welcomed into a host of establishments normally off limits,' he said.

'Her Majesty's Prison?' called out some aspiring lag.

'No,' rejoined the teacher, barely able to contain his annoyance.

Pub landlords, he promised, would bestow warm smiles of welcome. Smart trouser shop salesmen would offer to measure our inside legs, deferentially calling us, 'Sir.' Tough Palais doormen would perfunctorily nod to our burgeoning manhood as we filed into the thrilling world of the grownups.

'But none of this, absolutely none of this, will take place if one vital element is missing.' Our teacher paused. For the first time in all the years he'd taught us he finally had our attention.

What? What was it? Sex appeal? Muscles? Johnnies? Clean pants? came the tirade from the boys at the back of the classroom.

'No… Cash, you bunch of wallies. And what will ensure that you get that cash in shedloads?'

We hadn't a clue.

'GCEs. GCEs equals cash. No GCEs equals no cash. You don't have to be a mathematician to work that one out do you, Richardson?'

'No sir,' I ardently answered, not realising he was being ironic. 'But what if someone's a dummy, sir? Where do they fit in?'

'What if you are a dummy, Richardson? Well, there's always

factory work my boy, nothing wrong with that.'

Her Majesty's Prison suddenly sounded a palatable alternative.

Here was another incentive for me to unleash myself on the world of music. I loved music, but the sad truth was, I could do nothing else. The teacher's instruction on adulthood, and how it was waiting to warmly embrace us, gave me hope. We were, however, misinformed.

As soon as I was legally old enough to enter a pub I went in, clutching enough small change for a pint of something and three straws for my mates. No one told me that three straws in a pint wasn't bar-room etiquette. The landlord told me to bugger off.

The first time I visited The Palais I was ejected because I wasn't wearing a tie, and the bouncers stole the best of the girls we had gone to great pains to bring.

A trouser shop salesman ignored me when I offered to pay for a much-desired pair of tight drainpipe trousers with a Provident cheque, the poor people's method of payment.

'This is Fenton's. We don't accept Provident cheques here, sir.' He smirked as he pointed to the door. 'Try the Co-op.'

Go to the Co-op? Not me pal. The Co-op was for losers. Their trousers were for factory labourers. Still at least he'd called me sir. He'd done me a favour, for I vowed I'd make the grade. Worldwide domination and fabulous riches would one day be within my grasp. I would come back, buy the shop, knock it down and build a slum there.

The pub landlord did me a favour too, and the Palais bouncers. I hated the taste of alcohol, and I couldn't stand the smell of tobacco smoke.

Somehow I had to fit into this man's world. So one packet of part-owned Dominos (five ciggies each) and a deft borrow of my dad's matches when he wasn't looking, and I was away to sit with cousin Barry at the base of my favourite pear tree in Mrs Scott's orchard. I'd scrumped so many pears from that place she decided to put me in charge of the orchard to see if it improved matters. You know the saying, keep your friends close but your enemies even closer.

I spent half the morning fervently breathing in smoke, and the other half spewing out my breakfast porridge oats. I was desperate to learn how to smoke. The very idea of mastering that masculine skill generated heroic visions of leaning nonchalantly on the Palais bar, blowing smoke into the bouncer's face. After the second ciggie that vision began to fade, and after my third fag, I was so green in the face I could have camouflaged in the grass. By the fourth I had passed out completely.

Come the week's end I could do a passable impression of a human chimney. I discovered how to 'take it down' without throwing up: don't eat anything! In no time I shed a good amount of puppy fat, around a stone, but I also lost all my paper round savings in fag purchases.

My brother Charlie also had a paper round, but he couldn't resist keeping the money the customers paid him for the papers. He convinced himself, between picking up the papers from Mrs Hall's and delivering them to the houses on his round, that the papers had actually become his property, and thus the money he collected for them each week belonged to him. Such a broad understanding as Charlie's was not shared by Derek Hall, who began to quiz him on the alarming number of non-payers his takings book displayed. Charlie replied that the customers were simply not in when he called to collect. After three months, when his customer's papers were cancelled due to non-payment, the irate clientele stormed the village shop. Charlie was in deep trouble, and Dad gave him a good belting.

Our parents saved hard to allow Charlie to go on a school

trip to Switzerland, but he got caught with other ne'er-do-wells stealing from the hotel boutique, and the whole party were deported. The grubby incident was reported in the local paper and the guilty were all named and shamed.

If a leaf had blown over from the neighbour's garden, Dad would've returned it and apologised for the attempted theft. So, despite being his firstborn son, Charlie was kicked out. He was fourteen when he first went to live in his very own place, namely the coal bunkers by the station. I brought him the occasional loaf of dry bread which he would tear into. After a few days cooling off, Charlie was allowed back home, and that was the end of his life of crime.

Dad had quite a brutal side and Charlie perhaps saw more of it than any of us. Pete was my younger brother by five years. He and Raymond Paine, my rival's brother, started rifling through the trucks parked in the railway sidings at Ockendon station. 'Relieving them of their burden,' he would have called it. They nicked boxes of toys and hid the contraband in my dugout. My youngest brother Ian, at two tender years, wandered into the den a hundred yards from our house and discovered their wonderful stash of toys. Thinking it was Christmas he ran joyfully home brandishing toys and soft cuddly bears to show Dad. No prizes for guessing what Pete got for Christmas that year.

Weighing up the pros and cons, and not wanting to earn myself a good belting, I decided hard work would pay dividends. I worked hard from when I was around 12 until I was 18, when I left home to pursue my career.

Having said all this incriminating stuff about my brothers I want to state that they are now law-abiding sweet-hearted folk – and each year when I visit them in prison I let them know I love them very much.

OK, fine, that was a lie. Actually Pete and Ian followed my footsteps into the world of music. Pete played with the John

Dummer's Blues Band and later as drum tech for the Rubettes and Suzi Quatro. He is now a gifted singer and songwriter. Ian topped the charts in May 1984 with the singer and song-writer. Ian topped the charts in May 1984 with the Timelords, *Doctorin' the Tardis*, and co-produced Cher with Nick Coler, as well as writing stuff with Alice Cooper.

In his early twenties, after a succession of dead end jobs, my oldest brother Charlie met a lovely girl named Rita while on holiday in Spain, fell in love and moved with her to Ireland. With her help he found a great job, great friends, and his own true amazing nature, loved by many around Galway Bay.

Later in life we realise how deep an impression our early years make upon us, shaping or misshaping our personalities. The parents with whom we are gifted, and to whom we've been gifted, on whom our sense of security and well-being depended, often turn out to be the greatest thorns on our path to wholeness and completeness.

But to that I say everything can be overcome. Looking back I see that Dad really tried his best to do the right thing. I totally forgive him for how he was with me. I don't think Mum has a resentful bone in her body so whatever rotten things he did to her are also inconsequential history. We have all survived with a ready smile on our face and a song in our hearts.

Two

WHO WAS YOUR FIRST LOVE? Miss Cox aside, mine was my first pair of long trousers.

Until I was fifteen, my father insisted I wear short trousers. This wasn't the best news that could be administered to my long suffering, much laughed about skinny pins, which provided my school chums, and sadly the chummettes too, with a regular source of laughter and derision, such as, 'How d'ya keep balance on those drumsticks?' and, 'Did ya see those two bits of white string dangling down from John's shirt?' 'That wasn't string, that's his legs.'

Many painful scraps later, I owed it to my nobbly knees to protect them from this misery. My first long trousers, bought for me by my parents, were the lower half of a thick green tweed suit matched with a pair of Tuff Tom shoes, courtesy of Littlewoods mail order catalogue. Hardly the cutting edge in fashion, but gratefully received.

Then I overheard a conversation at school between Johnny Coppin and Edward Dennet. They were talking about some clothes that Eddie had nicked from Harry Fentons in Aveley, the store that wouldn't take my Provident cheque. Well, after the theft Eddie had been chased by the police into Daiglen Drive woods where he hastily chucked his booty, a pair of size ten winklepickers and some brown mohair trousers, as he tried to escape.

Feigning interest in Eddie's bravado, I admiringly asked about the route he'd taken through the woods on his escape, and armed with that priceless info, I dashed through the rain-soaked woods and found – joy of joys – a set of sodden wet trousers, hastily abandoned upon a bramble bush, and nearby some large black shoes smeared in mud. Despite their appearance, I felt like I was carrying the crown jewels as I ran back home.

It was not long before they were lovingly washed and dried, and although the shoes were three sizes too big for me, they were worn with great pride. The trousers were a little too wide for my liking so I got Mum to taper them. She had no idea they were nicked. I had also been taught by Alfie Biscoe how to do the spit and polish technique on my glorious long-pointed shoes, and in a few weeks I could actually see my face in them.

I was so proud, I wore them everywhere. Everywhere, that is, except home.

A year previously I had been on a week's holiday to Bedford with our next-door neighbours, the Nicholas family. The Nicholases were great. Mum and Dad both had good jobs and Terry and David, their sons, had five shillings (yes five shillings!) pocket money per week and all the semi-pointed shoes you could shake a hat at.

Anxious to improve in the footwear department, I found myself a pea-picking job on a nearby farm, and surprised my hosts by disappearing from the holiday house after breakfast each day and re-appearing around dusk with five shiny shillings in my grubby mits.

The Nicholases didn't stop me from working and were even kind enough to drive me on the last day from the quiet village where we stayed to the shopping centre, where twenty-nine and elevenpence bought me the finest semi-points that anyone in Ockendon had ever set their envious eyes upon.

On returning home I proudly displayed the twin works of art to my dad. To my horror he snatched them from me.

'Don't you ever let me see you wearing stuff like that,' he shouted, and threw them out of the front door.

If he would do that with a beautiful pair of semi-points, what would he do with winklepickers, especially stolen ones? At fourteen he ordered me back up to the barbers in the village and made them demolish the stylish haircut I'd had done an hour previously, in favour of a brutal short back and sides. Here's to teenage humiliation!

Dad, for all his faults, was honest. There were times when folk offered him a situation where he could earn money illegally, big money, and bless him (though I didn't at the time) he never went for it. He had principles. So I decided I would never let him see me wearing the winklepickers.

I hid my dubiously-acquired shoes and trousers in Alfie Biscoe's house down the street. Each morning I left for school in my normal attire, sprinted the hundred yards to Alfie's alleyway, disappeared excitedly into his shed and emerged a new man. On returning home from school I would change back to my short trousers and Tuff Tom shoes and no one was the wiser.

Alfie said the winklepickers were so sharp you could pick your nose with them. I replied that if I could pick my nose then I would've picked a better one. The trousers were so tight, you needed half a pound of axle grease to get them on. But get them on I did. I refused to take them off, even for school sports, and stubbornly wore them in every badly-lost race.

Despite the trousers I still couldn't get it on with the girls. Me and my friends never seemed to have the ready cash to get into the local hops where those lovely maidens tantalisingly sported. Then Courts, the modern secondary school in Aveley, started Friday night dances at two and six to get in. Two and six was more than any of us had, but I was determined to get amongst the action.

I climbed in through a seven-foot high window. The window was curtained, so the people inside couldn't see me. I had fastidiously ironed a razor sharp crease in my mohair trousers, but as I scrambled onto the space where the window opened, I bent my left knee to get a foothold and ...zing... went the crease, from knee to groin. I landed, minus one shoe, on the floor behind the curtain, with what looked like a pair of curtains hanging from my left leg..

I would've stayed hidden there till the dance was over and then slunk out, but fate and the Belhus bully boys had other plans. A fight had broken out in the hall. In a matter of seconds, a bloody-nosed teenager came careening into my curtain, impelled by the bully boys' kicks and punches, and followed by a gang of screaming girls looking for refuge. That was my lot. The curtain got pulled down and there I was, with my one shoe and split trousers, trying to look nonchalant. I knew I had to do something quick, so I fell on the boy who was nursing his sore nose, and aimed a couple of fake blows to his chest.

'Next time you won't get off so easy!' I yelled angrily, pretending he was responsible for my split trousers. Then, jumping up and dusting myself off, I beat a hasty retreat toward the exit, trousers flapping ridiculously and wearing one lonely shoe.

Around this time I had began to notice that more songs were written about losing the girl than winning her. One popular song by Neil Sedaka was called '*Why Must I Be A Teenager In Love?*' I could really relate to it and in response wrote my first ever song entitled, '*Why Must I Be A Teenager?*' I took solace from the fact that some of our songwriters at least had something in common with me. Instead of joining the hapless bunch of teens on the dance floor, and more rejection, I decided that I would play the music they danced to. So I tried my hand at being a singer.

I sung in my first band when I was fourteen with Geoff Archer, a classmate who played bass, and the Legg brothers, Ray and Colin, who were guitarist and drummer respectively. The brothers had their own small amplifier, and a mike that I could use to belt out the very best Marty Wilde, Billy Fury and Cliff Richard songs. Their dad had a good job, so the boys were blessed with all this nice equipment. Unfortunately, Colin, who played the drums, was not blessed with a sense of rhythm. The practice sessions on Wednesday evenings at Courts School were frustrating, as Colin ruined all our attempts to sound half decent.

I tried to help by showing him how to play the pieces – I already had some idea from watching drummers on TV. But Colin was struggling, and getting more and more frustrated with me, so I thought it wise to desist. Eventually Geoff and I split and formed another group where I took up the drums and Geoff, who had a bass but no amplifier, plugged into the back of our radiogram and chonked away.

Before I left home to try and make it as a professional, I played in a number of bands with Geoff, the best of which was The Gas Company. This band boasted a Burmese singer called Tosh. We played locally and around the Home Counties for a couple of years, until the group disbanded to seek individual successes elsewhere.

My parents, as you have already gathered, were always strapped for cash. When I was a teenager, Dad made it clear that if I left school on Friday, I should start my first job on Monday.

It was August 1963. I left school on the Friday and headed straight for the dentist. My teeth were bad and I had to get them fixed. I knew I wouldn't be allowed time off work for this, so I got them all done in one go. I was there for over four hours and the dentist, Dr Hodivala, gave me eleven injections. It was incredibly painful and by the time I got back home, Dad was in bed asleep. He woke when he heard me come in and called me into his darkened room. He could only see my outline.

'Where've you been?'

'At the dentist.'

'Liar! Your head and face are all swollen. You've been in a fight.'

Dad promptly went back to sleep.

It was only when I looked in the bathroom mirror that I realised my head had morphed into the shape of a football. I was shocked and more than a little sorry for myself. Mum wasn't there at the time. She was in a psychiatric ward due to a nervous breakdown, brought on mainly by the way Dad treated her. I feared the thump thumping of my daily drum workouts hadn't helped either.

The cocaine started to wear off, and I cried the night away in pain. Some years later the dentist Mr Hodivala was struck off the register for accidentally killing a man with too much anaesthetic. I guess I should count myself fortunate.

Actually, I do.

Before rushing on with my story, I should say a little about the music of my formative years, and how it influenced me.

We grew up in the post-war period with dance bands such as Cyril Stapleton and Humphrey Littleton, then Big Band Jazz, then Traditional Jazz with Kenny Ball and Acker Bilk (none of which even slightly interested me). Then came Skiffle, the precursor of Rock-n-Roll. Musicians borrowed their mum's thick serrated washboards (no washing machines then), a tea chest with a pole and string attached became a bass guitar, and a banjo (or any stringed instrument hibernating under Grandma's bed) completed the line-up.

Skiffle intrigued me. Lonnie Donegan was its champion, and his recording of Rock Island Line was my first purchase of a real live record and my first taste of heaven – a snip at 6 shillings and 8 pence. I loved them records. They whizzed around majestically at 78 revolutions per minute (my cousin Barry said he had personally counted them) and brought me unlimited joy with every rev.

Dad loved classical music. He bought a piano on the never-never. For a while he played it, his right hand playing the tune nicely, but his left hand not cooperating. Even at my young age I knew something was wrong, and his musical exertions never brought us much pleasure. Sadly, Dad's ability to keep up the payments was on a par with his left-hand piano skills, and the tallyman came and took the piano away.

Later dad got a piano accordion and was enthusiastic for me to learn it. I did my best knocking out *Oh Mine Pa Pa To Me He Was So Wonderful* (ironic) and *Saint Theresa of the Roses*. I wanted to show off my new-found skills, so I asked some boys and girls round to watch me dexterously knock out these tunes. Soon, however, it was painfully evident that they were laughing at me, and I realised that however well I might play it the accordion just wasn't cool. By the middle eight of *Saint Theresa* they had disappeared across the field with Mickey Payne and Johnny Barber to play kiss chase. Dad loved music, but after his abortive attempt to make a virtuoso accordionist of his son, he refused to help me some years later with the purchase of my drums, citing my rejection of his chosen instrument.

Each assembly morning at Benyon Junior school in South Ockendon, after prayers and announcements were over, a classical piece would play as we quietly filed out. I loved the Minuet by Boccherini, especially the bit near the end. I used to stand at the back so I could be the last to leave, hoping to hear 'the bit near the end'. When I did, it ran through my head all day, bringing with it pleasure and hope. Dad gave the school a recording of the Piano Concerto in B flat minor by Tchaikovsky so we could enjoy that too.

From a young age I was exposed to special music and unique melodies and rhythms. There were times when I couldn't get enough. Some nights when I would come home late from the youth club and Dad was already asleep, I would sneak over to his beloved record collection and play the sextet from Lucia Di Lammermoor over and over again. I defy anyone to find a more heart-wrenching choral piece than this.

Then came sweet Buddy Holly and *Peggy Sue* and I was not in post-war Ockendon any more, I was *Three Steps to Heaven*. My very favourite duo, The Everly Brothers, gave me *Cathy's Clown*, and bit by bit the die was cast in my soul that music would be my challenging saviour, friend, confidante and lover, and eventually I would spend more quality time in intimate accord with it than with anyone or anything on earth.

Oh sad modern world, where are the songs you could hum along to? Where has *Yesterday's Lovers* gone? I keep looking, but I can find no trace of you. Show me another Roy Orbison with songs of such intricacy and cadence as his.

Upon leaving school, persuaded by parents and teachers that a career in music was out of the question, I opted to be a journalist, having some love for the English language and getting to the bottom of things.

I got a position as general dogsbody in Reuters, Fleet Street, then the home of England's foremost newspapers. My job was to sweep up the discarded paper coming from the row of comptometer operators who were receiving news from all around the world, and to carry the pages containing breaking news to the other comptometer operators sitting opposite, who would then type up the news and send it off to press agencies the world over.

With most of it you could take your time and saunter across to the other side of the room every ten minutes or so armed with breaking news. However when an operator would receive news that was deemed a priority he would shout SNAP! That meant you had to get it across quickly. In terms of priority even SNAP was dwarfed by the word FLASH! That meant something earth-shattering had occurred. I think I only ever heard it once. I was so shocked that this special word of words had been called that I ran and grabbed the type from the out tray and fed it across to the other typists for a full twenty minutes before it dawned on me that I hadn't read what had taken place and that I should at least take a peek. When I got a spare moment I looked into the tray where they kept all the duplicates and saw the headline:

JOHN F KENNEDY, PRESIDENT OF UNITED STATES OF AMERICA, SHOT IN MOTORCADE IN DALLAS. SOURCES SAY INCIDENT WAS FATAL.

John F. Kennedy was everybody's hero. He was young, good looking, charismatic, bold, and almost as popular as the Beatles. He had stood up to the bullying Russian President, Nikita Krushchev, in the Cuban Missile Crisis, forcing the Russians to remove their secret nuclear missiles from Cuba. I remember I was in the fifth year at Lennards Secondary Modern in Belhus, Essex, and we were being prepared for the third world war by our nervous teachers.

I took the threat very seriously and purposely sat next to Marion Percy in class so that if the siren sounded, I wouldn't go to nuclear hell without a good snog first. Fortunately, Krushchev recalled the missiles, the world was saved, and so was Marion's chastity.

Anyhow, JFK was very big with us. So were the Beatles, whose music confounded the pundits, the record industry giants, and all the boring lack-lustre musical elite. Their songs weren't written for them by a bunch of suits in Tin Pan Alley, but by their own blessed selves. Nowadays, everyone has a poke at it, but in those days, barely any British artists wrote their own material, and the Beatles were a revelation.

At that time, only the upper class or the filthy rich would be seen driving a Bentley or a Rolls Royce. The Fab Four changed all that, and what's more they drove their cars with jeans on too. I was crazy for John, Paul, George and Ringo, and, like everybody else, I wanted to be like them. I tried my best the following year when I joined the Liverpudlian band, The Mad Hatters.

Alas, the job in Reuters was one of the greatest downers of my life. It was poorly paid – the price of my season ticket on the trains virtually halved my wages. It was shift work and I hated working nights. I had just started courting a lovely girl, my first girlfriend, Pamela Richardson (no relation, I hasten to add). My night shifts meant I hardly saw her and when I did I never had enough money to take her out, and we usually ended up at her place, with her mum as company.

Pam, however, had a nice record collection and educated my music tastebuds – my taste until then was pretty much music by Caucasian males. Pam turned me on to Ben E. King and The Drifters, opening the door to Soul music and later, to the likes of Otis Redding, Little Richard, Sam and Dave and Sam Cooke.

Four years later in 1967, with my wife-to-be Cherrille, I saw Otis Redding, accompanied by Booker T and the MGs, live at the Ramjam Club, Brixton. I think Cherrille and I were the only white people in the audience. As Otis effortlessly tore into one Soul classic after another, I remember holding Cherrille round the waist so as not to lose her in the heaving crowd. Otis's up-tempo Soul music had no comparison, except perhaps Sam and Dave, but it was his soul ballads that were beyond equal. He could take you to a place that was way off any map. When the opening line of *I've Been Loving You Too Long* issued from his golden mouth, he seemed to represent our deepest yearning for love.

Living in London, Cherrille got to see the Beatles at Leyton Baths and the Rolling Stones at the Finsbury Park Astoria. Every other Monday she would see Manfred Mann at the Marquee in Wardour Street, and John Lee Hooker at the Hundred Club in Oxford Street. I say see, for due to the tumultuous screaming at the Beatles and Stones concerts she never heard even a tad of the music, whilst this country bumpkin living in the sticks had to be content with listening to the records. When we were courting in 1967 we used to meet up after work and go to the music shop on the corner of Cambridge Heath Road which stocked all the American imports and listen to the latest cuts of Soul artists from the USA.

After buying Percy Sledge's *When a Man Loves a Woman* or *Stay With Me Baby* by Lorraine Ellison, we went up to her bedroom to play our new songs non-stop on Cherrille's little Dansette record player, and there we hugged and kissed, like kids to the soundtrack of our youth.

The Beatles' first album paid tribute to these early black recordings when they included *Chains*, *Mister Postman*, and more. McCartney himself said that among their early influences these hitherto unknown artists had a powerful impact on their own music making.

The first Motown tour of England in the 60s included such greats as The Supremes, Martha and the Vandellas, and Stevie Wonder. But they were so little known and appreciated that the whole tour was a financial disaster, with Berry Gordy, the founder of Tamla Motown, admitting that not one theatre was more than a third full. The Beatles, beside bringing into this world their own unique brand of music, were responsible in part for promoting the wonderful contributions of black musicians. The Stones were also great champions of these blues artists from the Southern States. But probably the greatest unsung heroes to champion the wonderful 'black invasion' were Alexis Corner and the jazzman Chris Barber, who both put there money where their mouths were and brought us Sonny Boy Williamson, Little Walter, Sonny Terry and Brownie Maghee, Howlin' Wolf, and many more. Those were the days, my friend.

My cousin Barry always remembered things that were lost in the fog of my own memory. If he were sitting next to me now, he would probably say, 'John? What about that dodgy old band Crusty and the Rave-ons that you did your first gig with back in 63? Why don't you write about them?'

'Crusty and the who?' I'd reply, and he would explain.

'You know, the band with that girl singer with the overbearing gay showbiz father.'

And I'd say, 'Blimey, the one whose orange hair swept across like a Bobby Charlton comb-over?'

'Yeah, he was ever so attentive to your needs first time you played with them at the Working Men's Club in Brentwood,' Barry would tease me.

'Whaddya mean attentive?'

'He'd stand at the side of the stage and run on and fan you if you started to look hot... He ignored his daughter when she asked him to change a microphone or turn the sound up or down. He would be too busy staring at you. And do you remember when they ran out of songs toward the end and Crusty asked her dad if they should start repeating some of the songs and he called out, 'Let Johnny do a drum solo!' And you'd never played a gig before in your life, let alone a solo.'

Yes, my cousin Barry would have remembered and retold

it just like that.

All I remember is coming home with 2 pounds 10 shillings, a fortune for a couple of hours work. I lay in my bunk bed, unable to sleep, as I replayed every moment of that set in my head; every beat, note and sensation in that paradise they called Brentwood Working Men's Club. So what if it was the only paid gig I did that year?

Dawn came around 4.30 and, without a wink of sleep, I rose, dressed and went to fold papers at Mrs Hall's newsagent. I'd be back around nine after finishing my paper round, and Barry's too, as I knew he wouldn't turn up after our late night.

Barry's parents both worked and he was an only child so they were relatively well off, had nice furniture and plenty of good food. When I got cheesed off with life at home I used to go to Barry's just up the road at number 12. He had every Buddy Holly record and we used to sit and listen to that music, dreaming our dreams and eating salad cream sandwiches. Heaven!

Barry's dreams came true when ten years hence he became a famous hairdresser to the stars: Mel Gibson, Warren Beatty, Donald Sutherland, Diane Keaton and Julie Christie, to name a few. I was not to know that my dreams would come true one day too.

Three

SOME PEOPLE WRITE NOSTALGIC SONGS basking in the halcyon days of their youth, like *I Miss the Hungry Years* or *Yesterday*, as though there was something there to inspire longing and outpourings of sentimental love. For me there was nothing wonderful or mystical about those times. They were hard and uncertain.

Looking back from a safe distance I remember, in 1965, working in Brown and Tawse's steel tube factory in Horndon. The factory had overhead cranes that ran on rails across the ceiling. I longed to break away from my dirty job of stacking massive greasy pipes for collection by the cranes onto waiting lorries. One cold day I thought I'd try to increase my respectability amongst my fellow workers, get noticed by management and hopefully improve my working lot.

In winter the open-ended factory was freezing. Everybody who handled the cold steel pipes suffered, so I decided to make my bid for personal glory and a crane job. I took advice from my dad, a trade union supporter, and he suggested I form our own union, which I did. Secretly. Then I boldly approached Mr Bean, the manager, on behalf of the lads and complained about the cold.

I had all forty employees signed up to my pretend union, and proudly informed Mr Bean that we were now a union and that we had rights. Flabbergasted that I had stolen a march on him, Mr Bean nervously fingered the lapels of his tweed jacket.

'So what is it thee are bloody asking lad?' he said in his thick Yorkshire brogue.

Hiding my joy at his tell-tale nervousness, I made my declaration.

'We, the members of (I made up some bogus trade union name) demand salamanders every twenty yards along the factory floor.'

Having demanded paraffin heaters, I said I would be in charge of lighting and fuelling them until winter was over. As some of my workmates began to assemble at a safe distance, Mr Bean eyed them disdainfully.

'Oh? And is there anything else I can do for Mr Richards?'

'Mr Richardson, sir. Now that you ask, there is something else. When winter's over I'd like the first crane job that comes available. I'll do it well. And of course,' and here I dropped my voice to a whisper so my workmates couldn't hear, 'I'll have less time to mix with the men on the shop floor and thereby not be influenced so much by their never-ending demands for improvements to their lot here...'

He said nothing, but an untypical half-smile appeared on his hard-bitten face, and on mine too. That winter we were warm as toast with our salamanders, and the following spring I had my crane job, high up above the cold factory floor. Heaven at last.

This was the winter of 1964, when the Beatles were well established on the world stage, and I was dreaming of joining them there with a group of musicians from the Beatles' hometown. They were an eccentric threesome called The Mad Hatters. Each weekend I'd shack up with them in Cavell Street, Stepney, above Tina's Café, then return home to Essex during the week and do the crane thing.

The Hatters were an amazing bunch of Liverpudlian musos.

I was their drummer and my idol was, of course, Ringo. They had ventured down south, where their drummer left them after a few austere weeks. They heard about me, and Austin, Joey and John had themselves a fired-up, ready-to-rock replacement. We were going to rival the Beatles.

The first few weeks brought no work and the boys were forced to steal food from Tina's fridge in the basement below the café. They would creep down the stairs in the dead of night to take pieces of steak and cook it over candles in their bedroom.

After several months we started to get work in pubs and working men's clubs. We performed regularly in the Magnet and Dew Drop on the Isle of Dogs.

One night, Billy, a work friend from Brown and Tawse, came along to see us play. He stood in the crowd, enjoying the show, until a fight broke out.

This was not uncommon in the Magnet and Dew Drop. The pub governor always asked us to keep playing during fights because it added to the drama. So, being the Mad Hatters, we did. But I kept an eye on Billy. He was from the West Country and wasn't used to the roughness of the East End. He neutrally observed the punching, kicking and bottling until, inevitably, he was dragged into the brawl and quickly knocked to the floor. I saw another colleague from the factory rush in to help Billy, only to be bruisily despatched in a backward trajectory through the swing doors to the gents.

Meanwhile, the band played on.

Thoughts crowded my head. What would I say to Billy about not fighting? I was up on the stage and they were down there fighting. They'd think I was a coward.

Then I realised I was the only Mad Hatter still playing. The other lads were searching for places to hide. Joey, the rhythm guitar, was crouching terrified behind my drums.

They could hide, I couldn't. I wasn't going to let anyone call me a coward at work. On the factory floor, being slagged about cowardice was a worse fate than death. Maybe I could hit someone and then throw myself down on the floor and pretend I was unconscious until the fight was over. As I was thinking this, I saw a big guy kicking Billy in the head. I indignantly threw my sticks down, jumped off the stage and thrust myself into the fray. I hit Billy's assailant with the hardest right my nine-stone body could muster, and to my amazement he went down like a sack of potatoes. Encouraged, I fought on crazily, flailing about like a windmill, until the mob turned on me, and I was kicked from one end of the pub to the other.

Glass broke, girls screamed, and moans of the wounded filled the air. Then, as if by miracle, the fight was over. The invaders retreated, all except the one I'd knocked out. I'd been kicked across the room and landed right on top of him. His eyes opened, he saw me and begged, no more! What was I to do? I managed to crawl off him, pretending I had plenty left to give. Fortunately for me, he staggered out of the pub.

I looked about. Bill and Robert, the gents swing door hero, were being attended to in the corner. Now it was finally over, I could relax a bit. Or so I thought. The brawlers had not all gone. I was aware of a broken beer bottle coming for my head, and then I was rescued. Our manager, Bob Wykes, all of five foot three but also an ex-commando, stepped in and saved my life. Amazingly, I didn't get a scratch on me.

I met my wife Cherrille on St Valentine's Day 1966.

I'd been drumming with The Mad Hatters and visited the Rose and Punchbowl in Stepney to watch the local heroes, The Disturbance, who were friends of The Small Faces. Jimmy White used to drink in the Rose and Punchbowl, and he could fight, duck and dive with the best of them. There were so many fights there that Jimmy renamed it the Rose and Punch-Up.

Terry King, lead singer for The Disturbance, sang like Stevie Marriot. I asked if I could get up to play my harmonica and sing *Early One Morning* by Sonny Boy Williamson. They graciously allowed me up and I tootled away on my harmonica, belting out, 'It was early one morning, I was on my way to school,' across the smoke-filled room. I got a real taste for being with that group and whenever I could I would get up and jam with them. I seemed popular with the crowd too. One day, unknown to me, Cherrille was among them.

'Hands off, he's mine,' she told her friends.

Cherrille told me some years later that they called me Overcoat, because one of the reasons they liked me was so they could laugh at my overcoat. I had purchased my first overcoat from Montagu Burtons in Chrisp Sreet Market in nearby Poplar. The shop salesman said the length of the coat, which nearly reached the floor, would be all the rage in a few weeks. There's nothing like being a trendsetter, I smugly thought, so I bought this ridiculous coat and wore it at each visit to the pub, thinking it was smart.

Some months later, when Cherrille and I met at Barking station for our first date, I was nonchalantly wearing the overcoat. This gorgeous brunette stepped off the tube train at Barking, smiling sweetly, and her eyes alighted on my overcoat.

'You are joking aren't you?' was the first thing she said.

'What do you mean?'

'That's what I mean,' she said, pointing to my coat. 'You're not taking me out with that on.'

I took off the offending garment, and with Cherrille on one arm and the overcoat tucked under the other, we proceeded to Romford Dog Stadium for our first date. Cherrille was never one to mince her words.

Not long after the brawl at the Magnet and Dew Drop, Cherrille and I were invited to a party on the Isle of Dogs. I had been reluctant to go as it was very near to the fight pub. We'd been standing with a young lady for some time. She looked somewhat bewildered so I for some reason I took her hand.

'Can I look at your palm?' I asked her.

One touch and I knew everything about her life: the breakup of her marriage, her child, it all poured forth. Cherrille was amazed. The young lady was amazed. (Sometimes, I am still amazed.) But I wished I could have foreseen what was going to happen next. After I read that palm, a huge man walked up to us.

'Are you John Richardson?'

'Yes,' I answered hesitantly.

'You were the one in the fight at the Magnet and Dew Drop, yeah?'

'Yeah...' I stuttered, expecting cold retribution to take place any moment.

'I want to shake your hand.'

'What?'

'That guy you hit? You know you broke his jaw in two places? He's one of the nastiest guys around. He hangs out with the Krays, yeah?'

My mouth was suddenly dry. The Kray family ran the London underworld at that time, and I'd knocked out one of their minders.

'Oh, thanks very much,' I said, pretending that breaking jaws of underworld minders was a daily occurrence for me. As soon as he walked away I turned to Cherrille.

'Let's get out of here quick before someone else comes to congratulate me.'

Speaking of palm reading and psychic phenomena, in August 1969 Cherrille and I stayed over with our friend Georgie Nash at his bungalow in Enfield. George was a pianist who I was writing with at the time. After bashing out a song in his front parlour, with Cherrille looking admiringly on, George suggested we try a Ouija board. We set the letters of the alphabet in a circle upon the table, and then each of us placed a finger on an upturned glass and asked, 'Who's there?'

The glass flew around the board at an alarming speed, stopping momentarily at one letter after another, and we tried to work out what it was saying.

After about fifteen minutes of this craziness we hadn't managed to put together one coherent name or word. Then I had an idea. Maybe if we wrote all the letters down, we might be able to see if there were some formations we were missing. So Cherrille was posted as scribe for the dead.

'Is anybody there?' I asked, and Georgie and myself sped off on another round of moves and letters. This is what Cherrille wrote:

Wkfghwaskcuttdemvjdsdnfsroccomarchegiano

Nothing, waste of time, and we packed it in.

I put the useless piece of paper in my pocket. Next morning, on the train back home, I got the paper out and something astonishing caught my eye. I could see the name Rocco Marchegiano. You had to be a fight fan, which I was, to know that this was the great boxer Rocky Marciano's original name.

When the train pulled into the station Cherrille and I were flabbergasted to see on the news board, 'Rocky Marciano Dies In Air Crash.'

I often experienced such inexplicable phenomena. My psychic awareness was never far away.

Eventually, when Cliffy Smeeth vacated the drum stool, I took over as proud 'sticks' for the Disturbance – minus my overcoat. In those days I was living rough in the East End. A well meaning friend, thinking to help me supplement my income, got me a job at Sun Tugs. I was glad of the extra cash, as I was still a struggling amateur musician. I had my steady girlfriend, Cherrille, and I wanted to be able to provide a little better. The docks, I was assured, were the answer.

Although the days of the flourishing London East India docks had by the early sixties been submerged in history, Sun Tugs in Wapping were still an important feature of dockland life, boasting the largest fleet of tugs on the Thames. Its stalwart team of small ships would pull the big ships into the Port of London from the Thames estuary. They also had a number of bonded warehouses alongside the river with cocoa beans, sugar and other raw materials stored in thousands of jute sacks.

One of my tasks was to check all the roofs after strong rainfall to make sure there were no leaks. If water was allowed to lay undetected on the cocoa beans, they would expand and explode. Fire risk was great. So each day I and another young lad searched the three floors for any signs of moisture. After a few weeks of this, my mate got bored and suggested that we take turns. One of us could stay on the ground floor and have a kip on the sugar sacks, while the other did the checking.

There had been a terrible downpour the night before and on the Friday morning that followed, I suggested that even though it was my turn to rest that day, both of us should do a thorough check. My friend convinced me there was no need: he would take thorough care and I should just snuggle up for the next two hours while he took the strain. I thought this was rather generous of him. Who was I to argue?

Little did I know that he simply climbed up to the next floor and promptly fell asleep on the cocoa bean sacks, not even reaching the third floor to keep his part of the bargain. After two hours he returned to wake me, assuring me that everything was absolutely fine and we should go for our tea break. And so we did.

The mess room, propped up on four stilts, was at the end

of the tow path, about 20 feet above the grey waters of the Thames. On the land side of the tow path was a ditch where ancient, rusting propellers from defunct tugs lay in rows like a maritime graveyard. We skipped merrily up the half dozen steps into the old wooden mess hut to watch the amusing ritual of the old boys' tea break.

They took their tea seriously. Much too seriously. Every facet of it was to us laughable, from the placing of their dirty, ancient, tannin-stained Coronation mugs upon the filthy wooden trestle, to the precise amount of time the tea had to steep, to the number of turns of the ladle in the oversize prehistoric tea pot to procure the perfect cuppa. Jock, a bullying Scotsman, was the foreman. He loved to instigate a quick card game after tea, but became abusive or threatening if he lost, and sometimes fights would break out among the men.

The following Monday morning was one of the worst days of my employed life. No sooner had we two jocular pals set foot inside Sun Tugs compound to report for 'work', than we were incredulously whisked off by an angry Jock to the managing director's office, where we were grilled as to our exact whereabouts and activities the previous Friday morning.

What, we wondered, had we done to deserve this treatment? Jock dragged us to the east window.

'Take a look o'er there,' Jock ordered. 'See what ye've done?'

Oh my goodness, did we really do that? The upper part of the the cocoa bean warehouse was a smouldering ruin, with hundreds of sacks of charred beans lying in rows. Were we really responsible for that? Yep, we were. No wonder they were angry.

I dared not admit to sleeping while I supposed my pal had been doing the check, and there he was, swearing black was blue that there were no leaks and that we'd done our job properly. I, on the other hand was keeping as quiet as I could and letting the flack fall on him, deferentially nodding whenever it seemed he needed me to.

Even though it could not be proven that we were to blame, the boss ordered us to do extra punitive work around the compound. He must have had some inkling that we were a couple of slackers who needed special attention.

He dismissed us with a threat that from now on we were being watched carefully. We walked across the cobbled yard, past the charred ruins of our sloth. This yard had seen hundreds of years of nautical history float up and down the grey back of Father Thames. I wondered if it had ever witnessed two such shameful idiots as us.

Then Jock was there, like a bucket of cold water in our faces, shouting again.

'Jones! Your extra duties today will be sweepin' the yard and clearin' the drains. You, Richardson, you'll be makin' the tea each day and Gawd 'elp you if it's no' reet!'

Every day after that, he was there watching as I ran up the stairs ten minutes before the tea bell rang to get the kettle on. He was watching as I came frantically running back down, seconds later, to fill it at the tow path tap when I had discovered it was empty. He was there again, looking at his Scottish watch, as I staggered up with the giant kettle filled to its spilling brim. But he wasn't there inside the shack when I panicked because I couldn't find the priceless ritual cups that they twice daily brought to the altar of their cussing mouths. He wasn't there as I made the decision to dispose of the bucket full of filthy grey water that was for some reason sitting redundantly beside the mess doors. He wasn't there when I decided I must quickly get some clean water to wash the cups that I still could not find.

He was still there though, standing on the tow path, as the tea bell stridently pealed out. And he was still there, joined by a whole posse of Sun Tuggers, as I energetically threw the dirty water from the top stair onto the propellers below. They were all there and all of them saw it fall with a strange crashing, cracking sound. I wondered if, in its long history, this tow path had ever witnessed such looks on the faces of its rugged watermen as when they watched the destruction of their beloved Coronation mugs, which had been soaking in the pail's murky waters.

Suddenly I was being frog marched to the guvnor's office, with Jock's hot breath scalding the back of my neck. In front of the boss for the second time, Jock was calling for my blood. The guvnor cast a roguish smile across my shuddering frame and whispered to the foreman.

'Give him the job.'

'What job?' I asked, not that it made a difference. I needed the money.

It was decided I was not to be sacked. Instead I was to be assigned to de-barnacling and tarring boats in the dry dock. It sounded innocent enough.

Next morning, equipped with heavy-duty gloves and a protective suit, I was put to work removing the immovable barnacles with a machine that whined, cussed, spat and threw me off balance from its sheer power. It had me trembling and sweating. Just holding on to it while it ground its menacing path through the barnacles was a super-human feat. But I needed resolve because I could not afford to lose the job – hellish though it was. After a week of being beaten, shaken and broken by Barnacle Bill, as they called it, I was told to tar the ship, which in dry dock rose fifteen feet above me.

I was given a pot of black, runny tar and a pole with a mop on the end, on which were only a few remaining fibres. That's when I finally realised they were doing a number on me. They stood on the dockside and pretended not to laugh as each attempt at tarring the boat met with abject defeat. The tar, with precious little to stay attached to, ran down the pole and dripped over my face and hands. Worst of all it ran up my sleeve. Within an hour, not a single part of me wasn't covered with the cold sticky stuff. It was impossible to get it on the boat and impossible to get off me.

The sacking on Friday came as no big surprise. I was freed from the trauma of the work, although the tar held on for several weeks, finally releasing its grip after a day-long soak at the Poplar steam baths. Losing a job was expected for me, because I was always dreaming of how to become a professional musician. But I had learned early in life that I couldn't function without money. If I couldn't make money from music, I had to make it elsewhere.

That summer, when I was nineteen, I got a call from Tony Thorpe, the guitarist from Wee Willie Harris's band, to audition for a professional job in the Cromwellian Club in South Kensington, owned by the wrestler Paul Lincoln, aka Dr Death. You can't know how it feels, unless you've been in that amateur/semi-pro situation, to gain entrance into the hallowed world of the PROFESSIONAL. I managed to get Geoff in on bass. Geoff, my old school mucker, and I would become PROFESSIONALS together. All we had to do was pass the audition, which we sailed through with the assurance born of youth.

Tony said to leave our equipment set up at the club, because we would be starting two days later. Wow! Our first proper paid job, a residency at the Cromwellian! As I strutted along the streets of South Kensington, smiling and smiling, I eyed every passer-by as someone who might at any moment recognize my stature, my coming of age. I called Cherille from the phone box on Exhibition Road and told her I'd got the gig.

'This must be the happiest day of your life,' she said. 'Let's celebrate with a curry.'

I told my Dad I'd got the job and I'd be leaving home for

the West End. I promised I would still pay for my room, and quickly disappeared from our second house in Ockendon, number 286 Daiglen Drive, never to return. Dad said it was the darkest day of his life. Funny, until then I had no idea that I was that dear to him.

I had overheard Tony say to someone on the phone that the Cromwellian was the megastars' watering hole. This boy from the sticks didn't want to ask Tony what watering hole meant, but I imagined a large waterhole under the dance floor, and when everyone was drunk the floor would slide back and the megastars would jump in, while we pumped out our unique brand of show-stopping entertainment. Flashlights would blaze and pictures of Mick, Paul and Bowie would be splashed all over the Sunday papers, with me somewhere in the background playing my drums and looking like a real cool PROFESSIONAL. Sad, but true.

We were to live in the heart of London. The boys from the sticks were gonna get their kicks and they would have their own pad in the raunchy old West End. Ours was a functional two bedroom flat on the third floor above the 2i's Coffee Bar on 61 Old Compton Street. These days if you go by there you will see a sacred blue plaque on the wall commemorating the site as the place where rock-n-roll started in the 1950s.

Playing at the Cromwellian was a great chance for me and Geoff, and living in the West End was inconceivably cool. On the floor below our flat lived two strippers, Danya and Tulie. Below them was a seven-foot wrestler, Texan Sky-High Lee, and below him two circus dwarfs called Trixie and Reg. The ground floor housed the coffee bar and in the basement was the historic club.

On the first night we were to perform at the Cromwellian, Geoff was missing. One panic stricken phone call later and I discovered Geoff had decided against this chance. I couldn't believe he was turning his back on perhaps the only opportunity he might ever get to show the world his stuff.

'Who's gonna wash my socks and pants?' was his excuse.

So we went our separate ways. He continued to have the luxury of his mum washing his socks, and I went on to wash my own socks, hoping that eventually I'd be able to buy new underwear everyday – every aspiring musician's dream. Geoff was a far better musician than I, but not greedy enough to pull it off.

At the last minute we got Lee Jackson (later to join Keith Emerson's Nice) to play bass. We dressed in black velvet Gothic tunics and high heeled buckled shoes, paid for by the Cromwellian management. We played all Tony Thorpe's compositions, and after three months we were inevitably sacked. It was nice while it lasted though. Tony went back to live with his mum and Dad above their sweet shop in Ongar, but I was desperate to stay in the West End where I felt sure there would be more opportunities for success. Swallowing my pride, I asked the owner of the Cromwellian, Paul Lincoln, if he could find me another job there.

'Yep,' he said. 'You can help Harry the Heart.'

'So who will I be playing with Paul?'

'Anyone who fancies you matey,' Paul laughed sardonically and walked away.

It was not a musical engagement that Paul had in mind as my next employment but a go'fer in Harry's bar. Harry the Heart was an outrageously camp bartender who ran the ground floor saloon for Paul. I was filled with dread. Not only was Harry known for his spiteful tongue, but I would also have to face the hundreds of late night revellers whom I had been showing off to five nights a week previously. I had to carry their drinks, empty their ash trays and have my bum stared at and occasionally pinched by the gay community who night after night thronged there.

Harry shared a strange dialect with David, his assistant.

Whenever they wanted to say something rude or secret about the clients, which was pretty much all the time, they spoke in code, called Polari.

'Look at that bona homa palone,' Harry would say.

'He's got nischt karts,' Dave might reply – and so the evening would go with a strange running commentary about everyone and everything. Then Harry would shout an order.

'More tonics, John darling.'

And I would have to squeeze through the crowds of patrons, who wouldn't move unless their shoes were alight. If I took too long Harry would shout again.

'John, where are you, you daft cow? Get that tonic here, before I do something to you that you know you'd love.'

Sweating with anxiety, I would cringe and try to push through the jam-packed crowd.

Tom Jones was a regular. One night a customer refused to let me through and Tom spoke up.

'Come on pal, let him get by. He's only trying to do his job.'

I really liked Tom for saying that. He was a gent, and phenomenal at pulling women. Every night he left with a new stunner.

Tony and his wife Serena ran the roulette wheel, located at the smokey end of the room, away from Harry at the window. I tried to get up that end whenever I could. Olivia Newton-John was a regular with her singing mate, an Australian called Pat Caroll. Somehow she heard I was good at choosing numbers for people on the roulette board.

'Hi mate. I've got ten bob on me tonight. Which number shall we put her on?'

This happened several times and, aided by my little magic, she always won. I dared not tell Tony what I was doing – he would have sent me back to Harry.

In six months at the Cromwellian I must have seen every famous musician on the scene, except for Jimmy Hendrix who used to frequent the Bag O'Nails. I did see Jimmy's drummer though, Mitch Mitchell.

Mitch arrived late one evening with a burly bodyguard who had too much to say for himself. Mitch looked like he was still wearing his stage clothes, a short Victorian military jacket; or maybe he dressed like that all the time. Angus Maquade, a professional boxer, was the club bouncer. He allowed Mitch in, but said his mate was too mouthy and denied him entrance. Furious at Mitch getting through without him, his mate went for Angus.

Instead of pushing him away Angus pulled him inside the foyer, where I was standing with Dennis Dean, a short but seriously hard Aussie wrestler. With cold-blooded military precision Angus ducked down, grabbed the minder's ankles and upended him. Like lightning little Dennis sprang forward and stamped on his head. The man who seconds before was screaming like a banshee was now sleeping like a baby.

Mitch stood over his friend speechless. I had come out of Harry's room for some light banter with the bouncers. Now I'd seen for the first time what happened when they went into action.

For a while I thought maybe Harry's bar wasn't such a bad place after all, then one night at the club Harry came over to me.

'John? See the gentleman in the corner? He wants you to go home with him.'

I brusquely declined the offer and Harry was furious.

'Look, John, just go to the corner with him and give him a little kiss, that's all.'

That was it, I'd had enough.They can kiss each other by all means but they're not snogging me. I threw the job in. Due to the resultant lack of cash I left my little flat and beat a hasty retreat back to the East End to continue musical apprenticeship.

Four

IT WAS JUST 1968 and I was twenty-one. My happy time spent playing with the Disturbance in the Rose and Punchbowl in Whitechapel had come to an end and now I went to join the Medium, who were the resident musos at the Nags Head in Hackney Road some four miles distant. Around that time I started to feel like time was running out for me. Kenny Jones, who was my age and a good friend of the Disturbance, had already scored his third hit in the charts by then with the Small Faces. And here was I still covering his and other successful groups' hits for peanuts. What's more, I was threatening to marry that beautiful buxom girl from Bethnal Green and I had to start showing her (and Tom her distrustful Irish dad) that I was worth something.

I got a small income from the Medium, boosted by working behind the bar on the nights we weren't playing. I also cleaned the toilets and, when the landlady was busy, changed her baby's nappies (unpaid). I was quite good at it because I used to do it for my adorable little brother Ian.

The lead singer of the Medium was Alan Williams, and the bass player was Mickey Gower. Mickey, like me, was into paranormal stuff, and one day we had a reading from a spiritualist medium. She predicted that Alan Williams and I would be famous and travel all over the world. At the time we pretended that it was the funniest thing we had heard in ages and fobbed it off though secretly we both hoped it would be true.

Our manager, Terry Hollingsworth, was a bit of rough diamond. In order to publicise our record, Colours of the Rainbow on the CBS label, he got us all into a rainbow-coloured dingy on the Thames. We were to pretend to be having a photo session on the river, with the photographer in another dingy. The plan was for us to 'accidentally' fall in, then Terry would jump off London Bridge and rescue us.

That was the plan. No one knew the current was so strong. We went in the water while our co-manager, Fat Les, watched from the bridge. He was supposed to run to the nearby phone box and call 999. Instead he started screaming.

'Help, help! Save our darlings, Terry! Lord, above, save them!' Then Terry did an amazingly heroic jump. By the time he surfaced and started swimming in our direction, we were being swept by the treacherously strong current way beyond the bridge.

'Terry! This way!' we shouted from forty yards downstream, as he began frantically swimming in the wrong direction.

Eventually Fat Les had to call the Port of London Authority tug to rescue all of us, including Terry. Fortunately it arrived quickly and we were duly rescued and taken to hospital. The nursing staff soon realised the whole thing had been a publicity stunt, not a genuine accident, and we got the full treatment, with bigger than necessary needles in the bum to counteract the effects of the highly polluted Thames water we had ingested.

They were happy times, I guess. Happy knowing we were gonna leave them behind us one day. We were skint and we lived a skint lifestyle, but I was doing what I loved to do. Cherrille and I were together again after a difficult patch. We were delighted to be back in each other's arms, and had thrown caution to the wind.

Then one day she announced to me coyly, 'John, I'm eating for two!'

'You're pregnant? I said to Cherrille, astonished, as though it had nothing to do with me. 'What will we do? You spent all our wedding money on dresses!'

'Oh,' said Cherrille, smiling coyly. 'I'll just let the dresses out a bit.'

Even though she'd spent the money she was always good at making do and if things got a little tighter financially than we could manage we could ask Enid, Cherrille's mum, if we could borrow ten bob till next week. She was always ready to oblige and often invited me over from my £3 a week flat opposite for the evening meal with the rest of my wife's family.

With a lot of hard work and frugal management of finances we saved enough to pay for a nice wedding and reception. On Saint Andrews Day, 30th November 1968, two and a half of us marched up the aisle of Our Lady of Assumption, Bethnal Green, and into yet another brave new world.

At the reception, after my initial nervousness, I found myself quite enjoying the occasion. All the nice things people say to you, the fuss they make. I did get some unwanted attention though.

'Now just pack in this music business, it's not going to work,' said my dad. For fuck's sake give me a break dad, I thought, it's my wedding day.

Then during a visit to the gents I was flanked by two of my father-in-law's Irish friends.

'You'll be taking good care of our Cherrille for us won't ye now, laddie?'

'Yes, of course.'

'We wouldn't want anything happening to you now. That would only upset our Cherrille, wouldn't it now, be Jaysus.'

They zipped up their flies in unison and went out without washing their hands. Blimey, I thought, who invited the Irish mafia?

Tony Thorpe, who played with me at the Cromwellian Club, provided the musical entertainment with his wife Shirley. He passed on a couple of jokes for my speech.

'Trust me, mate. These'll go down a storm.'

I trusted him, and after thanking families and friends for attending, got stuck into Tony's jokes.

'They say that every bride looks beautiful.'

'AAH...' breathed the guests as one in mute appreciation.

'So where do all the ugly housewives come from?'

'OOH!' they cried in disgust. Even Tony didn't laugh. I shifted from one foot to the other hoping for a change in my fortune, then cleared my throat. Now for my best one.

'I was born with a broken arm. I was trying to hang on till after the wedding.'

Deadly silence. Mum furrowed a quizzical brow.

As the tumbleweed blew slowly across the wedding reception hall I wished myself back in the gents with the Irish gangsters.

Before I was allowed to receive the precious hand of their Cherrille, the Catholic Church had insisted on coaching me for six weeks. Father Patrick tersely taught me how to rightly behave with a Catholic girl. But the first Sunday after we tied the knot, when I got ready to go with her to Mass, she refused to come. She said she'd had enough of the church, and could I give her a snog instead.

The same year, Arnold Schwarzenegger relocated from Austria to live in Crow Lane, Romford. Within a relatively short time, due to his determination and massively honed frame, he became Mr Universe. The competition was held in an unremarkable venue in North London. Had Arnold, once success was within his palm, left it at that, he would probably have been no more than a forgotten name in the annals of body-building history. But he saw other openings, and reinvented himself spectacularly.

I was booked to play with a band at the Mr Universe after-show party. An hour before the show, Arnold, God bless him, was showing off his ludicrously muscled frame, parading around the hall, daring us not to worship him. He let people touch and squeeze his biceps which he happily exposed to the rest of us under-developed pygmies. I found it all quite amusing but, because everyone else was doing it, decided to join the long queue of mortals waiting for a perfunctory squeeze of the god's bicep. By the time I arrived at his horizontally placed arm and its ludicrous mountain of bicep, I wondered how even two of my paltry hands could half encompass it. Quite unexpectedly, the bicep, along with every perfectly disproportioned feature of his arm, dropped suddenly to his side.

'You no touch.' he said, scowling at this nine-stone weakling. 'You have the long hair. No touch. No touch!' His English wasn't so good then.

Mr Universe obviously thought I was gay. And Mr Unimpressed of Bethnal Green thought Mr Universe was a twit, but on with the show!

An hour or so later we began our stint for the night, trotting out covers of the music of the day. The muscle-bound hulks began to grace the floor with their formidable presences, and I was reminded of an African watering hole at dusk. First, the lightweight and junior champions began to dance, then slowly heavier and bigger guys joined them until finally Arnie entered like a bull elephant. He went to the middle, scattering the lesser ones as he spun, gyrated and posed.

Just when I thought the evening was going to fizzle out and we'd be on our way home with our twenty pounds tucked safely in our pockets, one of the lighter weight champions, tired of being on the periphery, decided to make a bid for fifteen seconds more glory by jumping onstage and getting his gear off. Maybe it's just me, but I thought it was hilarious as one by one the body builders clambered up, stripped down to their pants and revelled in the glory of the audience's whoops and squeals.

Then, clutching a giant bottle of unopened champagne, Mr Universe stunned everyone with his entrance. Instead of leaping on stage, Arnie found the stairs at the side and sauntered into the spotlight, huge bottle of champagne in hand. He put the bottle down, and to the beat of The Stripper slowly and artistically got his gear off.

When he was ready to swing into his posing routine, one of his friends innocently went to remove the magnum of champagne beside those large undressed feet. Arnie, realising that if the bottle disappeared into the crowd it was not likely to reappear, took hold of it and, looking around for a safe place, spied the long-haired 'gay' drummer. Arnie put the champers behind the kit, looked sternly into my eyes.

'Sweetie, make sure nothing happens to this won't you,' he growled, and returned to centre stage to continue his strut.

After the show was over I packed away my kit. My silver Ludwig drums were stashed and last to go was the guitarist's Vox amplifier. I went back to the stage for the Idiot Check and saw the champers still there. All alone, unloved, abandoned. Being a compassionate person at heart, I wrapped it in an old jumper that I used to dampen the sound in my kick drum and swept it into my arms to take it to a well-deserving home.

'Look, lads! Look who wants to come home with us.' I pulled back the jumper and the four of us delightedly huddled around the opened back of the van, parked on the high road twenty yards from the hotel.

Pop went the cork. Champagne fizzed. Nervously I took the

first swig while each band member in turn took his place as lookout at the side of the van. Just as we were about to indulge in a second round of swigs, made even sweeter by their illicitness, Bob the lead guitarist called out.

'Quick, they're coming!'

I slipped the outsized bottle into the back of the Vox. I am grateful to this day to their designer for allowing space for champagne thieves to prosper undetected. I looked round the side of the van and my nervousness transformed into terror at the sight of three walking mountains looming towards us.

'Where's the bottle?'

'What bottle?' we said as one, standing rigidly over the spot where the champagne had christened the road.

'The one I placed in your safe keeping, sweetie.'

'I thought you'd collected it. When I went in for the last time to get the amp it was still there,' I said, pleased with myself because technically it was true.

Not having a word of it they pushed us aside and looked accusingly into the back of the van, whose interior light was fortunately not working (along with most of the other lights on the clapped-out Ford). One body builder swept up the amp like an empty cigar box (along with the hidden champagne) to see if it was buried in the pile of musical paraphernalia. None of them noticed the wet patch on the dry road. Dropping the leaking amplifier, disgruntled, the mountainous trio annoyedly lumbered back to the hotel. Nine Stone Weaklings, one; Twits United, nil!

The relief was overpowering and with the rest of the champagne summarily consumed, (as yer do), we drove past the hotel ten minutes later. Arnie and his gang were doing chin-ups on the hotel's sunshades.

Maybe it was the champagne, but I wound down my window and called out.

'Hey! Arnie!'

He dropped from the sunshade and waved.

'Hi!'

'Goodnight!'

'Goodnight!'

I don't know what he said in reply to my next remark as the sound of burning rubber may have muffled his response.

'Wanker!'

After a couple of years playing with the Medium I joined a group called the Pattern. I was still in search of my elusive pot of gold – even a basic wage would have been welcome – so I joined them to see if my fortunes would fare any better. The husband of the lead singer, Ayshea, was Chris Brough. Chris was in charge. He was public-school educated and unusually polite for a manager.

He landed a gig on Granada TV for the Pattern. We worked for thirteen weeks in Manchester on 'Lift Off with Ayshea.' And we actually did, at least for a while.

While we were on the show, we backed quite a few famous acts and met some very nice people. We met Kenny Rogers, who was just starting out with the First Edition. He sang *Something's Burning* and produced this amazing sexy vibrato in his voice. I knew one day he was destined to shine through, but I was not so sure about myself.

After the show we used to go round and sit in the empty Rovers Return bar and mimic different characters from Coronation Street. One day I sat with Barry Blue who was playing bass for the Pattern and we were taking the mick out of the different characters in the show when I heard a throat being cleared loudly behind me. Oops, it was Ken Barlow, one of the show's big stars, regarding us Southerners with unmistakeable disgust.

'Wotcha Ken,' I said. 'How's Deidre?' He walked away. I don't blame him.

Contrary to my hopes for fiscal advancement, it soon became obvious that Chris was as skint as we were. Not knowing this at the time, I used to approach him for financial help. We had done some work up in Yorkshire at Whitby Bay Yachting Club and I heard from the other group members that the money had finally come in. So I asked for my share.

'Dear boy,' he replied in his polite upper class voice, 'that money has had to be paid out for the insurance on the van to keep you and your dependants safe and secure should the unthinkable transpire.'

As I doffed my working-class cap in his direction, the little voice inside my head screamed, the effin' unthinkable has already happened mate, we're poorer than church mice.

By then I was married, subsisting in a dingey flat with our baby daughter, Pia, the pride of my life, born to us in August 1970. Pia was a very advanced baby. By ten months she was walking. By twelve months she was speaking quite freely and coherently, by eighteen months she was sitting at the table wielding a knife and fork, and by two years she was driving a fork-lift... sorry, parental pride running away with itself. Being a parent gave me a taste of deep love of the most blissful kind. More about Pia and her younger brother Scott later.

We lived in two rooms and a small kitchen, sharing a downstairs toilet. The saving grace was Cherrille's careful handling of our finances and her mum, who as I said lived in the flats opposite and from time to time cooked wonderful meals for us. I used to look forward to dinner at the in-laws.

I was still miffed at Chris's dismissal of our needs and wanted our posh manager to see how we lived in comparison to their upper middle class existence in Mill Hill, so I invited Chris and his wife Ayshea round for dinner one night.

'Skint, you say, Chris? Come to my place for dinner.'

They were unable to decline my invitation, and when they

came I could hear their gasps of horror. We had a springless settee given to us by Cherrille's boss, which even the cat wouldn't sit on. We had no heating or running water. Chris and Ayshea couldn't hide their shock that people actually lived in such conditions.

Five

I CAN'T STAND TALKING about all this failure. I want to jump ahead to happier times, so I'm gonna fast forward to sweet '74, even if there were more balls-ups to come.

When the Rubettes got to number one I went to Harley Street to get help with my knee.

Just before the Rubettes grasped fame, I was drumming on Barry Blue's touring show, which opened in Bolton Arena to two thousand screaming kids. The hospitality bar saw a little more of yours truly than it should have, and the upshot was that I jumped out of the tour bus while it was still moving, as you do. I think I could have managed the impact onto a passing grassy verge, but Geoff Daley the sax player jumped on my back as I was in mid-flight, and the cartilage in my right knee tore out. Somehow I managed to continue touring, using my left foot on the bass drum, and doing sessions in London, limping back and forth on the trains with my drum kit.

So as soon as the Rubettes and I could spare a moment, I had my knee operated on and attended a Harley Street physiotherapist, Mrs Roberts. Her husband had given the Beatles 'extra assistance' in a drug-related kind of way, and their song *Doctor Roberts*, on the *Revolver* album was written about him.

As I left the clinic after my first treatment, who was standing in the ante room looking very frail?

Keith Moon, drummer for The Who.

'Hello mate,' he said, offering me his hand to shake. I couldn't help seeing a massive slice across his wrist.

'What's that, Keith?'

'Oh, that? I was at a party last night – someone threw a glass up in the air and I tried to catch it.'

Yeah, sure.

He was very friendly and, would you believe it, seemed to know me. Maybe it was because we were in every paper and on every TV show on God's earth at the time, or maybe he was an expert bullshitter. He asked about the group, my knee, and many other things.

Keith wouldn't have remembered, but several years before, at the Revolution Club in Mayfair, he had bought a round of drinks for our band, the Medium, after he'd listened to our set. We had been bowled over by his kindness.

Outside the club we had been loading in our equipment when he drove by in his Bentley. He had fitted loudspeakers in the front grille and a microphone by the steering wheel, and as people crossed the busy street beside the club, he shouted endearingly at them, 'Piss off out of the way, you cretins!' and other such stuff.

People were shocked by his talking car. It was amusing to see him playing his tricks. He was great in his own way. Like the rest of us he fell victim to the massive excesses so readily available to us bunch of naive plonkers. Spliffs, dexys, uppers, downers, cocaine, heroin, LSD and my poison, booze – these were the muso's best friends.

It was only years later that I found out just how dangerous such frivolities could be.

Six

THE MOVIE OF LIFE HAS ITS OWN RULES – and you never quite know what's coming to a cinema near you.

Cherrille had always insisted I be there for the birth of our first child in 1969.

'We started it together, we're going to finish it together,' she said.

Personally, I was not that keen. In those days hardly any men were involved in birthing, but a promise was a promise. On the night Cherrille delivered, in the dilapidated Victorian maternity ward of Bethnal Green Hospital, there were at least twenty other expectant mums, waiting, straining, heaving, screaming and cursing.

I sat there holding Cherrille's hand, terrified. I wanted to be back in the Magnet and Dew Drop fighting The Krays with one hand tied behind my back – anything other than this.

'It's getting late. The baby doesn't look like he's likely to appear yet. I think I'll go home now and come back in the morning.'

'Sure,' Cherrille said. 'And don't bother coming back, you sissy'.

Only one nurse was on duty for all twenty women in varying stages of labour. She drew curtains round each one of the twenty beds as we prepared to face the prospect of a daunting night. Cherrille quickly became more and more uncomfortable, muffling the painful motions of the baby's downward journey with polite whimpers. Some of the other women were screaming out full-bodied expletives with not the slightest tinge of self consciousness.

The woman two beds down began screaming, 'Nurse! Nurse, please come! I'm going to have my baby any second.'

There was no response.

Cherrille started to groan louder and began squeezing my hand with a strength I never knew she possessed. Then her contraction decreased and she let go. The woman two beds down was not letting up though. I peered around her curtain like a frightened rabbit.

'Doctor, it's coming, help!' she pleaded.

I fled to the room where the nurse was comfortably seated, oblivious it seemed, to the unfolding dramas in the labour ward, and begged her to attend the distressed lady. I was summarily dismissed by her muttering something about how many centimetres dilated. I didn't have the heart to tell the distressed lady that the nurse was not coming. Shaking, I returned to my wife, not sure of who was comforting whom.

A massive scream split the air, followed by a squelching sound from two beds away, followed by a newborn's cry.

Obviously the solitary nurse, with a ward chock-a-block with labouring women, was well and truly out of her depth.

After two more hours Cherrille's water broke and I persuaded the nurse to give us some assistance. I followed as she pushed Cherrille in a grubby, paint-chipped trolley to the delivery room.

The baby took a long time to come. He was in distress, and jammed tight. The nurse seemed unsure of what to do. Several times she called a doctor, but it was in the middle of the night and no help came.

Finally our beautiful baby squeezed out, but although his little heart was beating, he didn't seem to be breathing. More frantic phone calls, and twenty agonizing minutes later a doctor finally arrived. He injected our baby in the heart but it was too late. Our baby was gone.

The whole surreal episode was doomed from the outset. My magnificent wife was so brave, but I felt we had been let down badly. I held our little baby, John, for a while, and tried to deal with it like I imagined a man should deal with such a thing. Then the nurse asked me to step out while she tended to Cherrille.

I went outside and sat down on the darkened stairs alone. As the tears flowed, I heard a voice from deep within.

'It's okay. What has happened is just,' said the voice. Instantly, I felt a sense of peace. My tears eased. I had the strength to go back in to be with my wife and support her in whatever way I could.

At that time I had absolutely no understanding to deal with such a shocking turn of events. I knew nothing about karma, the law of cause and effect. But those amazing words that were whispered into my soul that night had a deep impact.

Cherrille was always the stronger of the two of us. The next morning, when I returned to the hospital ward, she was sitting up in bed smiling. I looked around and noticed that all the other ladies had their beautiful babies nicely wrapped in cots beside them. Next to my dear wife was an empty space. I nearly burst into tears again, but choked them back down inside.

'Don't worry. I'm fine,' said Cherrille. 'When can we go home?

'I'll ask the sister,' I said, thanking God (whoever that may be) for the opportunity to be useful.

Cherrille is the kind of person you can always count on. Years later, in 1981, we had another stillborn baby, whom we named Karl. Again Cherrille was no-nonsense about it. She didn't want the children to hear the news from anyone but herself, she first wanted them to see that she was fine. Our dear friend Helen Perfect brought them to us at Harold Wood Hospital. The children bounced into the maternity ward with bright smiling faces, expecting to meet their new baby brother.

I don't know how we managed to restrain the tears within our broken hearts. We didn't want our two sweet sensitive kids to see us weeping. Cherrille spoke to them tenderly, telling them an accident had taken place and the baby had died shortly before in Mummy's belly, but Mummy was fine.

When I saw the shock and disappointment slam into them, I was unable to hold it any longer and burst into tears. Pia, who was just eleven, surprised me.

'Dad, don't cry. It's alright,' she said matter-of-factly.

For a short while we hugged and cried together, and I knew the worst was behind us and we could get over this, mainly thanks to Cherrille and Pia.

Some weeks after the tragedy, Cherrille revealed that when she had been six months pregnant she had visited a friend, Pat Burnham, who had recently given birth to a beautiful baby girl named Emma. Pat had raised Emma into the air, giggling above her, and a voice in Cherrille's mind had said, 'How are you going to deal with it when you lose this next baby?' She took this as a warning of things to come, but in typical courageous fashion never revealed it to me.

When the children had left with Helen for a pizza treat, I left Cherrille for a few minutes to find somewhere to cry again. I ended up outside behind some bicycle sheds, and let it all out. Exactly the same thing happened as before.

'It's ok. Everything is as it should be,' said a calm measured voice within my heart, and without another tear I returned to my wife's side.

In the early seventies I made my way into the exclusive realms of the recording world. I couldn't simply sit and wait to see if something would happen with the Pattern, so I tried hard to become a session musician. This was a jewel in the crown of any musician who was not already part of a famous band.

Fortunately, I had learned to read drum music when I was sixteen. This put me in good stead for this line of work, as most producers required their session musicians to read.

Being a session musician was hard work, but I was used to that. It meant good pay to sustain my wife and family, if ever we were to have one. Little by little, I started to acquire session bookings.

I worked with Tony Atkins, Nat Kipner and Barry Leng from ATV and Ron Roker as well as Barry Green, later known as Barry Blue with Gerry Shury.

Gerry was one of those rare folk who never got angry, always had a smile, always had the time and, fortunately for yours truly, always booked me. Tragically, he died when he was only thirty-two. His car just careened off the road on the way to Brighton, for no known reason, and he was gone. He was such a wonderful person that half the music industry turned up for his funeral.

At first, I started to do sessions for nothing, so that word of mouth would spread; the first vital step on the ladder. Because we couldn't afford a car, travelling to the studios meant getting a cab to the West End, playing the session and then returning. It cost about ten pounds for the round trip. I would do the sessions at a reduced rate just to be heard and appreciated, and just ask for ten pounds. Gradually word spread. 'Oh, you should book John Richardson. He's good.'

To truly arrive on the session scene, I was told, I needed a fixer, a sharp-minded businessman with all the important contacts for getting hopeful lads like me established in the top-paying bracket of session work. There were maybe two real fixers, and they had every big name artist on their client list, plus accounts with film and TV advertising agencies that paid handsome fees for the right musician's skills. The top fixer was David Katz. If you worked for him you could name your price.

It had come to David Katz's attention that I played every style around at the time and could read sheet music passably well. He left a message with Cherrille that my presence was required for a film jingle at Advision in Wembley.

When I heard the news I danced up and down the kitchen with my beautiful newborn son Scott held triumphantly aloft. This was the blessed moment any serious session musician dreamed of: to be one of Dave Katz's kittens.

The session was on the Saturday morning. On Friday I played two sessions, then stayed up late writing out a story for my friend Steve Kipner, who was leaving for Los Angeles the next day to deliver to his contact at the Disney studios. It was an opportunity I couldn't miss. Before midnight I drove to Cavendish Street with the manuscript, dropped it off at Steve's, and got back home around one in the morning. I left Cherrille a note to wake me up at ten o'clock, in time for my session at one, then fell into a well-earned sleep.

No sooner had my dream begun, it seemed, than it abruptly ended with Cherrille entering the bedroom with an alarmed note in her voice, saying something about time.

I wiped the sleep from my eyes. Again I heard her alarmed voice.

'John, wake up! Alan's on the phone from Advision. You should be there now. They're waiting.'

'What time is it? You stupid cow!' said a man who had just had the hard work of the last four years nullified in one fell swoop. 'You've finished me, you idiot!'

Of course, she wasn't an idiot. I was. I stumbled down the stairs, pulling on trousers, grabbing car keys and opening the front door, multi-tasking for the first time in my life.

I broke every road safety rule in the book that day, nearly curtailing the lives of innocent drivers, pedestrians, stray cats and anything that stood in my frenzied way – mounting pavements, jumping lights, cutting in, cutting out. Swearing, cursing, crying, thumping the steering wheel. By the record time I arrived at Advision, my rage had turned to shame. I had to face the forty musicians I had kept waiting, as well as Dave Katz.

I tried to make a brave face of it. I lugged my heavy drum kit across the studio floor, not to the disgraced silence or jeers that I had expected, but to tumultuous applause. Man for man they stood up from their seats and roared their approval.

Trying not to think that this had anything to do with me, I began setting up my drums. Ten minutes later, my trembling sweaty hands finally embraced the one thing I was any good at, thumping those skins.

As the film appeared on the screen above, we ploughed into the piece at the deft drop of the conducting baton, syncing the music to the visuals without a hiccup, thank God.

During the tea break I disappeared to the toilets, not wanting to bump into Dave Katz. Before long my name was called out over the tannoy, and when I reappeared into the throng of happy musicians it started again, but worse this time.

'JOHNNY, JOHNNY, JOHNNY,' they chanted, accompanied by clapping and cheering. Then Frank Ricotti, one of the best percussionists in the country, put his arm around me.

'Don't take any notice, they're only having fun,' he said.

'Thanks Frank, but why do they keep cheering? I thought everyone would be angry with me.'

'Double bubble, mate. You helped them all earn double money by being late. You're their hero.'

Oh my God... These sessions were already triple the fee, and now I had just cost the producers the extra time to hire this massive studio as well as double pay for all forty musicians. And I still had to face Dave Katz.

Now I was really shaking. I needed a miracle to get me through the second half of the recordings. I wanted to run, no, hide, no, die.

Two, three, four... We were in. Somehow I was playing, I was reading the music. But nothing meant anything. It was happening without conscious effort. I was stuck on auto pilot, and to this day I am not aware who or what switched me on.

I was the bad guy starring in a film about his life that the sound track was playing to. Even though I had never taken drugs, it was just how I imagined an LSD trip. The string section's arms were going up and down like clockwork toys. The conductor was a man from the lunatic asylum writing meaningless shapes in the ether. The tympanist was a mad cook thumping with stout clubs the monsters who periodically rose to the surface of a great copper cauldron with distressed cries of BOOM as their heads were firmly struck. The brass section were pumping out their cheeks like bullfrogs calling for a mate. And I was calling desperately for help. You think this is bad, said my mind, wait till you see Dave.

I thought of that old joke:

Q. What did the inflatable teacher at the inflatable school say to the inflatable boy who brought a pin to school?

A. You've let me down. You've let the school down. But worst of all, lad, you've let yourself down.

Crash! My right-hand stick thumped into the splash cymbal at exactly the moment it should do, indicating that whoever was playing my drums was now finished.

'That's a wrap,' called the conductor. 'Thank you, gentlemen.'

It was over. Back off the trip and planning my escape, my mind began directing its exit strategy.

Keep your head down. Dismantle that drum kit as rapidly

and noiselessly as you can. Dave is still up in the control room, quickly, do it!

Five long minutes later, kit dismantled and packed away, I was ready to go. At times like these I wished I'd taken up the flute. Gotta drag those cases as quickly and quietly as possible. Don't talk to Frank. No eye contact with anyone. Great… one more case and I'm out. Don't want the money. Won't stop for anyone or anything. Through the door, down the corridor, the outside world is only yards away. Nearly there…

God, I've got to put all this stuff down to open the door! Some kind soul pushed the door open for me.

'Thank you mate. Oh. I mean… Mr Katz.'

'Ah, John,' said Dave, flooring me with this unexpected greeting. 'A quick word if I may? Here's your money.'

He pulled out an already signed cheque from his immaculate suit pocket. I was filled with fear and shame that I had cost him thousands of pounds – and cost me and my family my career. It might as well have been a switchblade he was pulling on me. To make matters worse, I glimpsed that he had paid me the extra time too.

'Thanks,' I said. Oh shit, I thought.

'Your very first cheque from me, John.'

'Yes...'

He opened the door, looking me in the eye.

'I would like to say it's been a pleasure.' He paused for a moment. 'Yes, I would have liked to say that.'

He sighed.

'Goodbye.'

The door closed behind me, as did my top flight session career.

Mr Katz's sacred first and final cheque stayed in our sideboard for weeks. My mortification was too great to cash it. Eventually, two new tyres for my Skoda overcame my principles, and the cheque was history.

It wasn't long before my earning capacity increased. I got the bug for singing again, so around 1970 I had teamed up with Alan Williams, my old friend from The Medium, and we started writing songs, recording them as Baskin and Copperfield. We got a recording contract with Pleasurama Records, and John Kennedy, who had been the manager of fifties pop sensations Marty Wilde and Tommy Steele, offered to manage us. We were retained for twenty-five quid a week to write and record. What heaven.

In those days when the Beatles had albums out, wannabees like us thought nothing of dropping the songs we were writing to rush and cover the tracks that were not going to be released as singles.

John Kennedy had arranged through his contacts with Dick Rowe at Decca Records to have us record our first Beatles cover. Dick Rowe's greatest claim to fame was that he turned down the Beatles because in his opinion they did not have what it takes to make it. We were going to have a bash at the *Long and Winding Road* in his Decca Studios, West Hampstead, London. Desperately hoping we had what it takes. We'd never stood in front of an orchestra before. It was astounding. We were parked inside a circular recording booth with the mike hanging in front of our quivering lips surrounded by this massive ensemble of professional players and choral singers.

The fifty piece ensemble were booked for another act on the Decca label, Andy Silver, and just before they were about to pack up, Dick Rowe dropped them a couple of extra quid and handed out the sheet music for McCartney's classic. Before we knew it, Alan and I had our first record together.

We nearly had a hit with it too but unfortunately four other artists had the same idea as us. Airplay was shared by several wannabees, and our chance at fame duly fizzled.

Not to be deterred, we went straight back in the studio and had the thrill of recording one of our own songs, *I Never See*

The Sun, with the same fifty-piece orchestra. Pleasurama pulled out all the stops and bribed some DJs and producers on Radio One, the most important pop music station in the country. Plays on Radio One were like gold dust and often, to get a record into the charts, companies would resort to bribing both the producers and DJs of the shows as well as buying inordinate amounts of the recordings from chart shops. We had people travelling all over the country trying to buy the record illegally into the Top 40 Chart – almost all of the acts in the Top 40 were doing the same although no-one would admit to it.

Emperor Roscoe and a couple of other prominent DJs became favourably disposed to put our record on the playlist. Even with such favour, we were still just out of the Top 50. Then, as if by magic, we landed a place in the premier TV show, Top of the Pops. Flick Colby of Pan's People, the resident Top of the Pops dance troupe and pinups to a million adoring British males, routined Alan and I in Pineapple Studios. We were probably the worst movers she had ever had the misfortune to teach.

We turned up at Top of the Pops studio in our handmade clothes and our tinted long, flowing hair, thinking we were the bizzness. This was our big chance. It was going to go in the charts. One showing on Top of The Pops and we were guaranteed worldwide domination and fabulous riches, or so we thought.

Unfortunately, Alan, who was singing harmony while I was singing lead, was worried that his voice wouldn't be heard. He climbed up into the sound box, without invitation (it was really an out-of-bounds area), and told the producer to make sure his voice was heard.

As the orchestra struck up the opening bars of *I Never See The Sun*, we felt like a million dollars. We launched into the song, trying to look as cool and calm as superstars are supposed to.

We sped back in Alan's Hillman Minx to the East End, where we excitedly told the tale of what it was like, who we met and how much we'd drunk. We didn't own a colour television at that time, but our neighbour Mrs Arbour invited us to see our rocket to stardom at her place. We watched Tony Blackburn introduce us, and heard the opening bars of our song, *I Never See The Sun*. There we were, wide-eyed, me thinking, 'Hang on tight, here we go!'

Alan on harmony, me on lead. But horror of horrors, all you could hear was Alan's voice, while my voice, singing the melody, could hardly be heard. My heart sank and my bushy tail drooped.

'Please put my voice up a bit,' I prayed aloud on Mrs Arbour's settee. 'Up a bit, just a bit. Put it up. Pleeeeeez!' But all I could hear was Alan's voice pealing ardently over the top. To make matters worse, I was holding my mike further away from my mouth than I should, trying to be cool.

Cool it wasn't.

From that moment I knew it was over. Our record never saw the sun. It hardly even saw the light of day. I left Mrs Arbour's under a dark cloud. At that time, records that appeared on Top of the Pops for the first time always went into the charts, but ours was nowhere to be seen. It didn't even make the Top 100, and we were dropped by our record company.

I was informed by the powers that Beeb that all videos pertaining to Top of the Pops had either been wiped or lost and hardly a show remained from the 1970s. Imagine my surprise when, nearly forty years later, dozing on our comfy couch half watching Top of the Pops 2, I heard Rob Bryden's distinctive Welsh brogue introduce two lads named Baskin and Copperfield whom, he said, were later to become the leading lights in the Rubettes glam rock band. I sat bolt upright and watched me and Al strut onto centre stage with all the arrogance and surety of youth.

It was spooky, like seeing myself in another life.

Seven

BY 1972, WHEN I HAD REACHED twenty-five years old, I was doing sessions, playing the odd lounge gig, and drumming with a band called Smile. They had a residency at the Top Rank, Watford. We were employed there for two sessions, one pop session on Saturday nights and another session on Wednesdays for strict tempo ballroom dancing. The band was a nine-piece combo with four brass players, a keyboardist, guitarist, bass guitarist, drummer and vocalist.

Saturdays were good – the DJ took the first half and Smile the second. We played to around two thousand kids on one of those stages that turned 360 degrees like in the London Palladium.

Wednesdays, in contrast, were boring, as we had to play that awful dance music, sometimes to as little as half-a-dozen snobby couples. As I trundled each Wednesday night up the M1 in my trusty Skoda to face the music, the words of Don McLean used to ring in my ears:

I will not be part of her cocktail generation,
Partners waltz devoid of all romance,
The music plays and everyone must dance,
I'm bowing out, I need a second chance.

In those days, ballroom dancing was stuffy and boring,

nothing like the joyous display of dexterity and creativity it is now. Unlike Don, though, we couldn't bow out just because we needed a second chance. We needed the money. So there we were ting-tinga-ting-tinging away at The Sheik of Araby, Red Roses For a Blue Lady, and on and on, for the pleasure of a few couples gliding around the massive dance floor that on Saturday nights was filled with thousands of dancers.

'Geoff, too slow!' or, 'Geoff, too fast!' they cried indignantly to the bandleader as they swept past the stage.

As they ponced around the place in their reverie, the couples, lost in oblivion, sometimes bumped into each other. When this happened they would freeze and wait, and wait, and wait a bit more, holding their poses, until one couple gave in and begrudgingly moved off. We found out that this strange ritual came about because the first couple to move off would be made to look somehow more ungainly in extricating themselves. I used to spend the set scanning the half-lit, mirror-balled dance floor, yearning for a crash.

Smile was the band that taught me to drink like a real man, and during the break I drowned my sorrows in a not inconsiderable quantity of alcohol. They also indulged in a fair daffy of drugs too, but I was totally disinterested in doing that. Lager was my poison for playing live gigs and LVTs (large vodka and tonic) were my preferred tipple on sessions.

This particular evening, the area manager was going to pay a visit. Even though we loathed the job, we couldn't afford to lose it. We were tipped off by the bar lady that he would be sitting with the manager just above the stage in the executive box. Geoff told us in no uncertain terms that we must play well and act according to the circumstances in a formal, well-turned-out manner. We should be wearing our bow ties and tuxedos, he said wrily, (looking specifically at me) instead of the tee shirts and slacks that had 'started to appear of late'.

The box was empty for the first set. As we swung round on

the revolving stage to go for our break, we concluded that he was probably not coming, so we began reverting to our usual obnoxious behaviour backstage, cussing and filthy joke-telling, accompanied by copious amounts of ale-downing . I exaggeratedly pulled off my tuxedo and bow tie, chucking them in the corner, and we sat around in a circle of chairs passing both time and wind as heavy boozers are wont to do, till the second dismal set.

The customary spliff got passed around. When it got to me I'd always pass it on, deaf to the boys cajoling me to 'take a toke.' This time I did something I've never done before or since. Maybe it was the relief that the area manager hadn't turned up, coupled with the boredom of strict tempo. Whatever the bizarre reason, I took a massive suck of the joint, and the second time it came round did nonchalantly likewise, while continuing to sup my fourth pint.

'Five minutes!' Geoff called. 'Showtime, lads,' he added, slipping on his smart band leader's blazer.

'Sure thing, Geoff,' I said, hanging back so I could go down the stairs behind them all without my tux and ridiculous bow tie. To say the journey down two flights of stairs to the stage was the hardest thing I'd ever done...is a massive understatement.

Imagine legs previously fully co-operative to every directional command for twenty-four obedient years suddenly striking out on their own, at their own pace, in their own direction, without a word of warning. It's a big shock, to say the least. Trying to reason with these hitherto submissive servants was futile. My worm-like legs had turned, and in all the wrong directions. Gravity however at this point was still on my side and, aided by my hands which were as yet unaffected by this anarchy, dragged me down via the banisters to the stage area.

Now the panic set in. I didn't know what was happening. I

had never had an experience like this before. And I still had to get up onto the drum rostrum. My fairweather friend gravity who had ably assisted me down the stairs was no longer there to help, leaving me with no option but to drag myself like an inebriated tortoise across the bandstand to the drums. The others were taking no notice. Chris Rea our guitarist saw me crawling and laughed, thinking that because I was wearing jeans and a tee shirt I was trying to keep low so Geoff wouldn't see.

I enlisted the help of a rarely seen individual named superhuman effort, with his comrade in arms, blind fear. They hoisted me onto the drum stool. My hands and arms, though doing a passable imitation of limbs belonging to an India rubber man, took a resolute hold of my lower limbs and yanked my right foot onto the bass drum pedal and my left onto the hi-hat cymbal.

My head will clear any second now, I consoled myself. It's probably only a minor stroke or something. Duh. I still hadn't realised it was the spliff combined with the booze that had rendered me incapacitated.

My head was having a problem staying up. Oh shite, just let it loll forward, no one can see you playing right at the back.

Only the people in the posh box above the stage...

What did you just say?

Yeah just them people, who look like – THE MANAGER AND THE AREA MANAGER!!!!!

No time to speculate. You're a drummer. Do what a drummer does. Make it up. 1, 2, 3, 4 – came the dreaded count in.

TING TINGA TING TINGA TING TINGA... responded the drummer rather splendiferously I thought.

Lifting my head, filling with confidence, fixing that godlike area manager with my proud gaze I proceeded, ting tinga ting tinga...

But something did not feel quite right. The brass section kept looking over their shoulders at me and I responded in the way that I had been taught when you had made a mistake in the playing; just look purposefully at another of the musos, intimating it was them and not you who fluffed it. I did this but the guitarist and bassist also started to cast accusing glances as I continued to smile challengingly at the managers' box, daring them to find the tiniest fault in any of us.

But yet that still, small voice seemed to be urging my attention toward something. My gaze fell on my feet. Horror of horrors. They were not even moving.

Oh well, thought I, ever the optimist, I'll sort that. Sorry lads, here we go... Boom chick boom chick... See? Sorted. Bass drum and hi-hat reporting for service, SIRRRR!

Then I looked up and saw that the TING TINGA had gone AWOL. I'd got my feet started but my hands had stopped.

Hang on a sec, just a minor adjustment necessary here...

I continued on, oblivious to the devastating effect I was having on the music I was supposed to be leading, and to the disgruntled dancers coming by one by one to shout complaints and insults.

By this time I had entered the world of oblivion, that world where there is absolutely no introspection, where one is totally MAD and is convinced that everyone else but you is off the planet.

It was told to me by the other boys later how, in desperation to keep all four limbs playing, I abandoned the idea of doing what a proper drummer does, which is to play each limb independently, and just started playing the same thing with each of them.

First, apparently I tried TING TINGA TING with everything but after a bar or two I tired of that and reverted to playing everything as four beats in a bar with, it has to be said, very little aplomb. Even that's too kind. It was just CRASH

CRASH CRASH CRASH.

Then, I have it on good authority, even that became too much and I reverted to one massive SMASH per bar. Apparently I looked very pleased with myself on achieving that. Smirking at the world which lay at my feet, I was LACOOT: Loud And Confident and Out Of Time.

Amazingly, the boys forgave me. Perhaps they wanted the sack.

My next gig was also a most spectacular balls-up. Frank, our bassist, who also played with Cyril Stapleton's orchestra, offered me a job with Cyril's small combo, playing at the Hotel Piccadilly in Manchester on the weekend.

I had played well and Cyril wanted to offer me a regular spot with him for subsequent bookings. I agreed but made it clear that I could only manage the small group and not to ever book me for his fifty-piece swing orchestra which I was absolutely no match for, to which he summarily agreed.

The next gig I do with Cyril was at Cowley works Oxford, where they make the Morris Minor car, and blow me blinkin down it's the effin orchestra and bleedin Cyril didn't even give me any time to prepare. He managed to avoid me entirely until we were all on stage, all fifty of us, about to start two hours of music that I didn't know, didn't like and couldn't play.

As I played, I remembered the Dave Katz fiasco and I thought as follows. Let Dave Katz tell everyone what a useless waste of space I was, let Jock make me scratch barnacles with my bare fingernails till I begged for mercy, let Dr Hodivala inject poison in my mouth all night, and let Dad send me to school in short trousers until I'm sixty. But don't, please don't make me go on stage with Cyril bleedin' Stapleton's Big Balls-up Band, to die the public death of all deaths.

No one was listening, as Johnny lamb-to-the-slaughter Richardson sunk without hope into an ocean of shame.

One good thing came out of it though. I met Pete Townsend's dad, Cliff, before we went on. I did my best to make a good impression on him before he saw how bad I was as his drummer. After the show one of the musicians approached me with a benign smile to ask if I was alright. I told him honestly I'd never played so badly in all my life.

'Oh I'm sure you have,' he replied and walked away.

My life took a turn for the better with the arrival in this world of one of the warmest and sweetest persons on this planet. My dear son Scott was born in Hackney's Salvation Army Hospital in 1972.

He didn't immediately breathe or cry as Pia had. During those first few unbearably tense seconds the memory of the tragedy of our first baby loomed, and I was frozen in fear. Then the lovely West Indian ward sister stepped in with some no-nonsense clinical procedures and - praise the Lord - he took his first breath and cried the tears of a living breathing child. That was probably the only time in our lives when we were desperate to hear the voice of our child crying. I was so relieved I burst into floods of tears.

'Look Lord, he's crying the tears of joy,' proclaimed our heroine of a ward sister, and so I was, while Cherrille remained quietly triumphant.

When I could I got my old partner in crime, Alan, onto the sessions I was doing. He picked up reading music quite quickly and, like me, what he could not get his head around he bluffed and got through without too much hassle.

At the time many producers would get older, more experienced people (like us) to play and sing on their recordings, then put their teeny prodigies on the television to mime to our work. The kids would become the band even though it was not really their music or their voices. We didn't feel bitter about it – we were pleased to have the work.

One record I played on in 1973 ended up selling in the multi-millions, yet we only received the basic sixteen pounds session fee. In fact, all the musicians for that recording worked for almost nothing. Gerry Shury, the arranger, booked around ten of us, mostly from Smile, the band I was playing with at Top Rank, Watford.

After successfully completing the regulation three tracks, and on the verge of packing away our instruments, Biddu rushed out.

'Lads, please can you do me a huge favour? Can you slip in an extra track, pur-leeeze?' Who could say no to those big, beautiful pleading Indian eyes?

Then, with the musical parts distributed in a trice, a young singer boldly stepped forward. Karl Douglas sang a capella:

Oh oh oh ohhhhhh... Oh oh oh ohhhhhh...

We all corpsed to this corny starting line, but Gerry firmly admonished our impoliteness with a tick, tick of his baton.

'Gentlemen? One, two, three...'

Everybody was Kung Fu fighting...

The rest was history. The only professional recording I ever did for absolute peanuts, and it sold eight million copies worldwide.

Just before Christmas 1973 I got booked for a session with Polydor. It was for a massive nine-piece rock-n-roll outfit called Showaddywaddy, who had won the New Faces TV talent show, hosted by Hughie Green. There were two drummers – one was Henry Spinetti, a top session drummer of the time. It was an honour to be playing alongside him. They were trying to emulate the massive Phil Spector productions of the early sixties with two drummers, two pianists and many other musicians creating a wall of sound.

I overheard the producers saying that the session singers had not turned up and, seeing an opportunity to painlessly extract another session fee from our producers, approached the producer.

'Look, you've got us here anyway, why don't you let us see if we can do the backing vocals to your music?' Alan and I had grown up through the rock-n-roll era and knew only too well what was required. Having nothing to lose, they gave us a try. Several effortless hours later, we left the building with double pay in our pockets.

By Spring 1974 I had resigned myself to the fact that I was going to be a session musician for the rest of my life and would never be famous. At twenty-six, I considered myself too old. Many of my idols from the early days, like the Small Faces, were now on their second wind, teaming up with Rod Stewart, and I had not even drawn my first breath, so to speak.

Destiny, however, had other plans.

One of the rejected Showaddywaddy tracks that we'd played on the previous Christmas was getting airplay on the radio. The song, a pastiche of *Little Darlin* by The Diamonds, was written by Wayne Bickerton and Tony Waddington. It had bom-shoo-waddy bits, falsetto vocals, and I provided the talking bits, trying to imitate the guy who spoke on the Diamond's 1950s hit:

'People, take my advice. If you love someone, don't think twice...'

The track was called *Sugar Baby Love*. Polydor, feeling it had hit potential, put it out regardless of the fact that there was no actual group to front it. I wondered who the group that got it would eventually be. It couldn't be Showaddywaddy because they were busy recording their debut album with another record label. Would it just be a bunch of pretty boys?

Due to the large amount of plays it was notching up I thought it was bound to be a big hit. Even without a band, it had already reached number 51 in the national charts. But there it stayed, refusing to move up or down.

Andy Stevens at Polydor rang me.

'Guess what Johnnie boy? The Rubettes have been offered a vacant spot on Top of the Pops to play *Sugar Baby Love*.'

'Wow. Who's going to be the Rubettes, then? Have you told them yet?'

'I'm telling one of them right now.'

'Who, me?'

'Who else? I want you to do it, John. You played and sang on it. And if you're up for it, I want you to bring Alan and four other guys who would suit the gig and get to the BBC's White City Studios by 10am on Wednesday.'

Knock me down with a sausage.

Top of the Pops? Me? Unbelievable. My own record, my own choice of band mates, an appearance on the biggest pop TV show in Europe with a record that's played without any bungs, and a bona fide place in the charts.

You can't scream because the kids are asleep. You can't pinch yourself to see if you're dreaming because you can't stand pain.

Go to the mirror, check the face. Any spots? No. What about wrinkles? Mmm, makeup'll hide that. Yep, you could pass for twenty.

'Don't you ever stop looking in that mirror?' said Cherrille.

'This time it's different. The mirror's looking at me.'

'Why would the mirror want to look at you?'

'One reason. I'm success in the making.'

'Yep, I've heard that once or twice before.'

'Seriously, Cherrille. I've just been speaking to Andy Stevens.'

'Polydor Andy Stevens?'

'Yep. He wants me to appear as one of the Rubettes on Top of the Pops this Wednesday.'

'Well done. You can celebrate by doing the washing up you promised to do earlier.' She blew me a kiss and went off to bed.

I spent the next two days visiting and calling up the new members of the band. By Wednesday I had safely ridden the wave created by the initial euphoria. Cherrille's sweet, flat response to my excitement, coupled with memories of our last Top of the Pops outing with Baskin and Copperfield, got it all back into perspective. It's a session, just a session, but a paid one.

Deep breath in, out, in, out.

'Just off to the session, darling,' I managed to say as I left for the BBC studios.

'Bye-bye,' came the familiar loving call from the kitchen. 'Don't have too much of a 'session' afterwards. Remember you're driving.'

Driving off towards my destiny, I had time to think about how I'd set the whole thing in motion, and whatever would be would be.

I'd called the boys who played on the record, Pete Arnesen and Alan, and I tracked down a few of my session friends. There were two bass players I had to choose between and I found them drinking in the Elm Park Tavern. They agreed to toss a coin three times to see who would get the job. Mick Clarke won the toss. So we got the group together very quickly: Alan, me, Tony (from the Cromwellian) on guitar, Pete and Bill on dual piano, Mick on bass.

Rushing down to Top of the Pops later that morning we went via Oxford Street to see if we could find some clothes that would give our group an identity. We saw some white Gatsby suits and caps in the window of Take Six and, ignoring Tony's pleas that they were a tad fey, we snapped them up. We were already late and there was no time to lose. Flying out the door with our new found identities, we sped onto our next destination, laughing about how we, all serious rock musicians, were prepared to stand in front of the nation and sell our souls unashamedly for our sweet *Sugar Baby Love*. Such is the lust for profit adoration and distinction.

Why call yourself Rubettes, I hear you ask? Okay, so *Sugar Baby Love* was inspired by *Little Darlin*, recorded in 1957 by the Diamonds. Like *Sugar Baby Love*, their song had a speaking part, a falsetto part and an underlying *bom-shoo-waddy-waddy* backing vocal. Polydor were gonna call us the Rubys based around the precious stone idea. To make matters worse, a number of fifties groups had the appendage -ettes, such as the Ronettes and Corvettes. We too got appendaged-up, and Rubys became Rubettes.

My cousin Barry, the scrumping hairdresser, met us at the studio and spruced us up a bit. Some of us were too big for the white pants, so we had to cut up the restroom's towel roll and sew the extra material into the seam at the back.

We camped up the Rubettes' presentation by throwing in lots of Shadows box steps – they had been our childhood heroes – along with other corny movements and over-the-top gestures. We enjoyed our day out, not to mention the alcoholic beverages supplied after the show, courtesy of Polydor records.

After my last disastrous visit to Top of The Pops, I was expecting very little from the appearance. We basically forgot about it and went back to our jobs in our various pubs and clubs. Then each Tuesday, when the top 50 chart singles were announced, we were called by Andy, who informed us where the recording was placed.

The week we appeared, 51.

A week later, 27.

The week after that, 2.

And then…

Eight

NUMERO UNOHHHHHHHHHHHHHHH!!!!!!.......

Sugar Baby Love was number one! The thrill of that mid-morning phone call from Polydor's Andy Stevens was something I would wish on everyone.

Just imagine, you've been out till late playing a club for thirty quid. You're exhausted, and woken by the bedside phone at just the right time (around ten) by the friendly voice of your manager.

'You're at number one mate.'

Not only number one, but in order to get there, we had knocked Abba's *Waterloo* from its premier position.

That call repeated itself pretty much word for word at the same time for another four weeks as we beat the opposition off for one whole month. Scott was too young to grasp the significance of his Dad's success but Pia, who by then was nearly four years old, was excited to see her dad mincing up and down on the TOTP stage, rubbing shoulders with rock-n-roll history.

She was a musical child and had been in love with the Osmonds since she was two. She could speak, I might add, with a very convincing American accent. Nightly she'd have me tell her stories of how she and Donny saved the world or escaped some danger. She would play herself (with an American accent) and I would have to play Donny. Mostly, as I remember it, she was saving Donny from some dark forest animal or getting help for the Osmonds when their tour bus broke down in the Amazon.

So there we were, catapulted by the Lady of Fame, who had mercifully tired of our sufferings as we played strict tempo on a Wednesday night at Watford Top Rank. She thrust us into overnight fame.

First, though, we had to become an actual group. During that year, the record went to number one in almost every country in the world, and sold about eight million copies. In the twelve months that followed we had three songs in the top ten. We were riding high.

Unfortunately, after only a few months I got pissed off with it all. I wanted to enjoy a nice, peaceful karmic cruise down Easy Street, seeing as that we'd worked so hard to get there.

However, the peace and contentment I yearned for was conspicuous by its absence. I started feeling stressed, mainly because we didn't really have a manager and I had to deal with all the negotiations. Things were tough, and I found myself at odds with people, arguing about this percentage or that contract. To make matters worse, the boys chosen for the group were turning out to be strong-willed, idealistic, stubborn characters (somewhat like yours truly) possessed of a strong faculty for quickly forgetting their humble backgrounds. In short we had six chiefs and not an Indian in sight.

It was extremely tense. So, after flying first class all over the world to appear on TV and at champagne receptions, the euphoria, as is the nature of the human psyche, rapidly wore off and we had to get down to the hard work of being an actual band. To achieve that, we had to purchase a massive PA system, a giant pantechnicon to transport it, and hire crew to hump it, set it up and work it. Then, at the end of the year, we had to go out and prove to everyone, including ourselves, that we were a real group, not just a session group. That was an interesting experience.

Every musician knows that the tedious bump and grind of travelling is part of the territory. Sometimes we travelled for a whole day just for a one or two hour concert.

I found it particularly trying because I never felt comfortable in the air. I would love to be able to embrace the Goddess of Sleep on the long journeys to India, America and Australia, as some fortunate souls do.

In our heyday, we were flying abroad three times a week. After a year we decided to hire our own small twin prop and fly out from our local airport, Southend-on-Sea. Though every flight on civilian aircrafts was in First Class, the novelty soon wore off, and so the change to private aircraft was most welcome.

Roger was our regular pilot and he took Alan, our lead singer and aspiring Biggles, under his wing as co-pilot. At first it made me uncomfortable knowing that Alan was learning the ropes and poling the kite, as aviators say, while our tender behinds were strapped inside the aircraft.

Not able to find the Goddess of Sleep, I took advantage of the Demon of Booze instead and quite effortlessly forgot about Alan's apprenticeship in avionics and my own surfeit of aerophobic temperament. Whatever I might say against booze, it was still the only thing that could make me fearless on a flight, especially a bumpy one.

However there was one flight which really tested the merits of the bottle of Southern Comfort I had clutched to my bosom throughout the memorable journey

Everything seemed to be going well until we began to cross the Alps and hit this mother of all storms (though I've never worked out why it's always the mothers who should be blamed).

We were travelling in Roger and Alan's favourite plane, a Riley Dove. It was a ten-seater and the pilots sat in an enclosed cockpit. The two of them would wax lyrical on its handling qualities and how it was a joy to fly.

When we hit this storm I was praying that the plane still 'handled like a dream' as much as they said it did. Personally, I didn't believe a word of it – it was an old crate as far as I was concerned.

We were in the up and down draughts, zooming up a thousand feet in seconds and then plunging. The cloud was so thick and dark I could hardly see the wings. I consoled myself with the fact that we had two stoic lads at the pole who would fearlessly guide us through this terrifying ordeal. I got as much of the Southern Comfort down my shirt and trousers as possible, regretting not having got drunk earlier so I could face this interesting paragraph on the last page of our life in a jocular manner, like Sarge, one of our financial managers who travelled with us. This time he was singing a Scottish lament that his Glaswegian friend Zinky had taught him when he was living in the Gorbals: Oh I'll no-a want to bide awaah or I'll no-a wanta see you. But I'll come back to see yersall, yea I'll come back to see ya...

Seeing as it was impossible to get drunk before my death I joined in with Sarge and soon all of us were singing/screaming this Caledonian pre-plummet dirge.

If it was possible to add to this tumbling, rumbling, lightning-bolt strewn terror, hailstones the size of billiard balls (I kid you not) joined in the melee, just for the craic, pouring down upon us relentlessly from the heavens. The hailstones created a sound like Keith Moon destroying a luxury penthouse hotel suite with the sharp end of his pick-axe sledge hammer. Its roaring and pummelling upon the fuselage struck the fear of the condemned into our hearts. The sheer force of it all entirely stripped the paint off the nose cone, and took all the remainder of my hope for survival with it.

I focused on our intrepid pilots and tried to imagine them seated at the controls steering us away from spiky mountain peaks with unparalleled dexterity. I envisaged them acting cool, calm and collected, checking dials, plotting courses, casting amiable unruffled glances at one another as though it was simply all in a day's work for them.

God bless their stoically British stiff upper lips, I thought.

Then came a massive drop and another big thump as we suddenly levelled out from the next sky-dive which was so hard it burst the cockpit door wide open, and we could see our pilot-heroes.

They had let go of the dual controls and were holding their hands against the windscreen to support the beleaguered windows which were also taking a supreme pulverizing from the hailstones. Jesus. They're not even driving us. They've abandoned all hope. We didn't know that in such a situation, the pilot leaves the plane to 'trim itself', thus the hands off the controls scenario. But if we were scared prior to the door flying open, now cruel fear had us as frozen in our seats as the spiteful hailstones continued hacking us down from the skies. And our captain and first officer had abandoned us to our fate. At a time like this, who do you get in touch with? Why, it was enough to make any man religious

Just as I was about to dive forward to grab the controls which were whipping back and forward and turning wildly side to side like a rodeo bull's horns as they try to dethrone the rider, the storm was gone.

Oh, now I've got me started on dodgy flying stories I can't stop me'self.

I've always found it fascinating how different folk deal with impending disaster.

Below is an interesting tale highlighting this.

In 2000, I was visiting a flood relief site in Orissa, India that

I and a number of Seventies artists such as our Rubettes, Suzi Quatro, Showaddywaddy, Dave Dee, Boney M and New Seekers had been supporting. On the way back to Calcutta from Bhuvaneshwara, we hit some strong turbulence. It was interesting to see the similarities and differences in the way we all dealt with the incident.

India has over a billion inhabitants. It has dozens of languages, hundreds of dialects and religions. Never was this so clearly demonstrated to me than at that fraught moment. Next to me was a Muslim gentleman who started praying out loud to Allah. Next to him, a Sai Baba devotee started chanting *Sai Rama Sai Rama* In front of us were two Sikhs with resplendent blue turbans saying very rapidly, *Wahe Guru Wahe Guru* Some English ladies were laughing hysterically at first and then started shouting as the laughter turned to tears, OhmyGod! OhmyGod! And if that wasn't enough there were some Buddhist monks moaning something virtually inaudible yet very intense. For the occupants of the Indian sub-continents, it's second nature to take shelter in God.

The company we hired our first private flights from were called Fairflight. After a few arse-testing journeys we re-named them Scareflight. Reverting to the Scareflight years, we once appeared in Munich on Top Pop, Germany's premiere music show. This time Roger, our main pilot, had a mate with him from British Airways who fancied coming away for a weekend break, so Alan had to sit in the back. It had been snowing heavily and we were lucky to be allowed to take off into the dark snow-bound night for the 3 hour flight to England. I'd got myself nicely tanked up, as I didn't want the weather to steal a march on me.. After only 5 minutes of flight, still climbing, the co-pilot who'd come away for an easy break, started shining his torch onto the front edge of the left wing and then hurriedly whispered something to Roger.

Alan, the lucky sod, was already asleep beside me and I had

no-one to ask what they might be up to. Then the co-pilot did the same shining his torch on the right wing, and this time the captain looked intently at the illuminated area and then spoke urgently to someone via his head set.

Next thing I knew, Roger banked to the left and the plane started losing altitude rapidly. Naturally, I asked what was going on. He replied calmly, 'We're just going down.'

'I bloody knew that already mate, but why? Are we landing? Or crashing? Someone tell me something!'

I could clearly see fear in the co-pilot's face as he turned his head sideways to check the wings again.

'There's a build up of ice on the leading edge of the wings.'

He said no more and continued his frantic checking.

'Won't the wind blow it off?'

'Look,' he shouted with a mixture of fear and exasperation, 'No. It fucking won't. If it builds up much more it'll change the shape of the wings and then we'll become aerodynamically unstable.'

'What's that mean?'

'We'll be more like a stone than a plane.'

The cloud cover was very low, maybe 150 feet, and as we finally dipped below it, suddenly I could see the runway lights welcoming us back to snowy old Germany. Dozens of steaming fire engines followed us as we bumped gratefully back down. Alan was still blinkin' asleep. I quietly fumed with envy.

My aerophobia flared up unwittingly once on a flight to Nice. We had just finished a TV appearance in Paris and we had to get down to the Cote d'Azur for another show that night. So, when we took off, Roger told us that to get there quicker we should fly higher where the air was thinner, and then we could go faster. I wasn't listening to the rest of his talk about the oxygen masks. I went off in a reverie about thin air and was trying to visualise the difference between thin and fat air.

The up-shot was that because we were at an altitude where there was less air, the boys started taking regular draughts of oxygen from their masks and then putting them down beside their seat. I didn't think that was right. Surely we should have actually worn them, not taken a swig and then put them down. So I purposefully put mine on to set the proper example and started taking deep breaths thinking I had it right and it would only be a matter of time till they all followed suit and donned them. Besides, I liked the kind of wartime heroic pilot look that I imagined I'd assumed.

After some time, I began to feel uncomfortable and it seemed like there was a heavy weight bearing down on my chest. I thought I wasn't getting enough oxygen, so I started to take even bigger gulps of the stuff.

A little further along and now my cheeks began to feel like they were caving in and my jaw was tightening. Quick, more gulps. My fingers and hands started to involuntarily bend inward, making my hands look like deformed claws. Very strange. So cutting a long, pitiful story short, I thought I was a goner, and alerted our manager, Roy, that I wanted to lay on the floor because I was dying.

All these faces were looking down at this cretinous shape on the floor, and poor Roger had to make an emergency landing at Montpellier. They gave me even more oxygen as I lay there and I remember saying to Roy, 'Please tell my wife and kids that I love them...'

Minutes later we touched down. Bloody hell, I thought, I hope I've put clean pants on this morning. I'm off to l'Hopital des Frogs. Please God let me be unconscious if they have to take my trousers down.

French paramedics lifted me in one deft movement into the back of their ambulance muttering unintelligible French-speak except one line which sounded like, 'Oh, la la! C'est John, le cloune de les Rubettes.'

I thought, yes that's right, I am a clown. None of the others got sick. There's something wrong with me. After a few preliminary tests the head paramedic said something that Alan translated into, 'you've got too much oxygen in your blood, mate.

I quickly warmed up and de-cretinised, relieved that I wouldn't die ugly in France, but embarrassed that I had been killing myself with oxygen and created such a stir.

In the end I was fine - after a quick stroll around the airfield perimeter with a brown paper bag over my clown's head.

Once we had three massive hit records in so many different countries, the only place we could languish was on the front page of the many music papers and journals. That seemed the only place where we appeared to be relaxed, happy friends having a good time.

I had dreamed of being recognised on the street. Now we were recognised everywhere, even in motorway services at four in the morning. We'd been playing way up North and were eating an early breakfast in the Blue Boar motorway restaurant on the M1, when a young couple sat down on the table next to us and started to whisper to each other. A funny thing when you are famous is that the general public think you can't hear what they're saying. They babble on about you, sometimes saying very personal stuff, oblivious to the fact that there are two large ears situated either side of your head.

'Ere, look at the size of his nose.'

'Dunn 'arf scoff his grub quick.'

'Hark at him going on and on, he could talk a glass eye to sleep.'

The best one that night was, 'It can't be the Rubettes, they're eating chips.'

Life was just as hard as it had ever been, but at least we

were getting paid ten times more than a few months previously.

In the spring of 1975 we embarked on our first British tour, opening in a theatre near the seafront in Cleethorpes. The theatre was old and well in need of demolition but the audience were young and vibrant.

I couldn't wait for the moment when I came out from behind the obscurity of the drums at the back to sing the B side of our first hit, *When You've Fallen in Love*, to three thousand adoring fans. I arrogantly slung an acoustic guitar round my neck and approached the mike. Tony, our lead guitarist, was a competent drummer, and sat in for me as we launched into this Buddy Holly pastiche.

I was singing well, flailing the guitar at every moment I could for good measure. Right when I thought it couldn't get any better, I was proven correct when a plank below my stamping right foot disintegrated beneath me, with the instant result that my right leg disappeared into the void below the stage. There was a scream from the audience as if they thought it was a stunt; I had the reputation of being a joker. Jumbo, our drum tech at the time, came and pulled me out.

Pride comes before a fall.

Back then we had a French Morrocan called Eno Saada as our agent in France and we worked for him most weekends for a good number of years. Then quite unexpectedly, the gigs stopped coming in. We were surprised because the French public couldn't get enough of us. One month went by then another until six months later we were completely bemused by our predicament.

Then one day our manager showed us a writ from the Mayor of Britanny calling for the Rubettes to pay tens of thousands of Francs for losses incurred at his carnival when

Benyon Junior School football team, Ockendon
(me bottom row second from right, my dad back right)

Me (on the left) feeling less than inspired
as general dogsbody at Reuters

The House of Usher with Tony Thorpe and Roger Sutton, in 1967 when we were performing at The Cromwellian

The Medium, with Alan Williams and bass player Mickey Gower – resident musos at the Nags Head in Hackney Road, in 1968

Cherrille and our kids in our 'lucky' house, 1973

Little Scot outside our lucky home in Goodmayes. In the background is my Skoda, survivor of a thousand scrapes.

Me and Alan as we were during our Baskin & Copperfield period

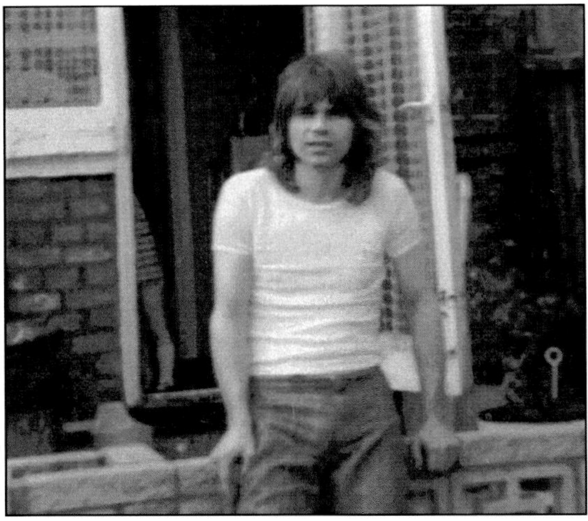

Just after the operation on my knee in 1974

Micky, Alan and moi on tour in France in the Daimler

The day we were thrown off French television
by wotsisname

Alan and me in Belgium for a press conference

POLYDOR LDN
POLYDOR 65522F
TELEX NR. 6054 LE 21.11.74

ATTN. ANDY STEPHENS

FURTHER TO MY PREVIOUS TELEX REGARDING TV RUBETTES

PLEASE NOTE THAT THE DIRECTOR OF THE SHOW WILL GIVE THEM

ON THIS NIGHT LIVE AND BROADCASTED THEIR FIRST FRENCH GOLD

DISC FOR 'SUGAR BABY LOVE'.
PLEASE CONVY THIS INFORMATION TO THE KIDS .

VERY BEST REGARDS

DANIEL GOLDSCHMIDT

The news of our French Gold Disc, 1974

Giving a concert for the President of France,
Giscard d'Estaing, in 1975

Waiting backstage with Bill Hurd

The Rubettes in 1975 at the height of our success – left to right from top: Mick Clarke, Bill Hurd, Tony Thorpe, me, Alan Williams

The Rubettes and Abba on Salut de Copains, Paris 1976

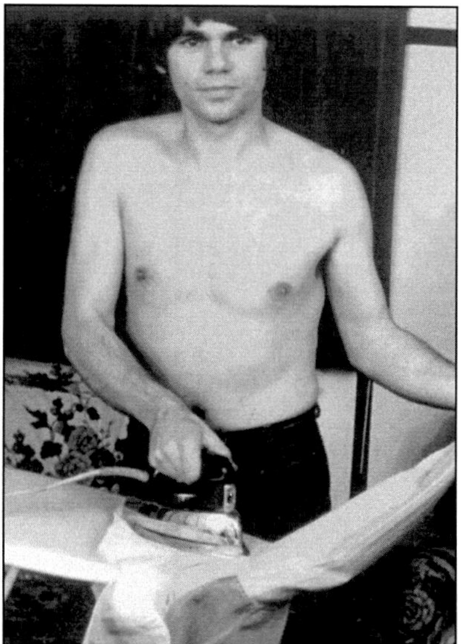

I even ironed my shirts after I became famous

Giving a party for the kids, around 1974, Pia on the piano and Scot on drums

The opening of our little herb shop 'Perfect Health' in 1980

Posy picture for new age recordings in 1983, the start of my collaboration with the New World Music label

Oh no! Back to the pubs again with Ken Gordon and Mick McCartney, 1985

Me and Alan

Charity gig at a pub in East Ham, with Gerry Slattery and Pia in the 1980s

The Rubettes singing A capella *in Belgium, 2010*

Pia, now Gaurangi, chanting in London

Receiving my initiation from my spiritual teacher, His Holiness Sivarama Swami at the Manor in 1989

Bhaktivedanta Manor, home of the Krishnas in Hertfordshire

Me in reflective mood outside the Krishna Temple in Soho, 2010

A member of the conspiracy of love

Chanting with a different drum at the Yoga Barn in Bromley

we failed to turn up for a concert we had been booked for.

Roy our recently-appointed manager checked our date list and then his contract files and said in his broad Dagenham accent, 'Luv a duck, something fishy's going on 'ere, lads.'

We'd never seen a contract let alone notification of this concert.

Roy asked for the Municipal office in Brittany to provide us with the contract we had supposedly signed, which they promptly did. But it did not show Roy's signature as it should have, it was instead scruffily signed, the Rubettes.

Roy called Eno who emphatically claimed he had no idea how that contract had been signed and said he would conduct a high-level inquiry. Fat chance.

Then it became clear that our dear, darling Eno had been doing this all over the country for the past six months. He'd book us into gigs without telling us, secretly and illegally sign the contract, then the night before the Gala, he would call the French promoter and say that he was terribly sorry, but the Rubettes had let him down, got sick, weren't answering the phone, had broken up or whatever, and the only thing that he could suggest was that they should take one of his other bands to save the show. All of the promoters fell for it and Eno sold his own bands to the desperate entrepreneurs because 'the show must go on.' All that is, except for the canny Mayor of Britanny who would not be fobbed off with one of Eno's naff overpriced French groups. If it hadn't been for the Mayor suing us, he'd probably still be doing it to this day.

It cost us more money in court fees to defend the action than we would have earned playing for them so let's just say that we lost. We were also pretty much finished in France – no promoter would trust us. Eno had seen to that. But cruel fate was to see to him a year or so later. I do so love karmic justice.

The group then played on the Belgian border of France. We

hadn't been able to get booked in France after Eno, but were still managing to bang a few out in Belgium where news of our unreliability had not yet spread. After our sound check we went to the Holiday Inn to rest for a couple of hours before the performance that night.

Arriving at the hotel with our roadies - five tough lads who had been consistently with us since the start in 1974 - we noted that there was a wedding in full swing in the reception area and they were at the stage of having the group photos done. When the wedding guests saw who was passing by with their guitars they began to call to us to come and have our pictures taken with them. Alan obligingly stepped forward, followed by yours truly.

The bride directed Alan to stand on her left next to the bridesmaids and the groom welcomed me as I positioned myself next to the best man and we began smiling and posing. Then Jumbo, our broad shouldered lighting tech, starts shouting to me, 'John, John! Look who's next to you!'

At first I didn't know what he was on about, then he pointed accusingly toward someone in the group and shouted, 'It's your friend.'

Confused, I turned to the right, and there right next to me was...

'Eno, how nice to see you.'

Buzzing at the speed of light were the options open to me now we had that little monkey, that very monkey responsible for eating all the bananas in our jungle, all the nuts in our forest and scoffing the hard earned fruits of our success. But it would be hardly appropriate at some innocent French couple's wedding: 'Excusez moi, just a second while we murder the best man.' I continued smiling through gritted teeth, thinking how best to serve the thieving chimpanzee.

Eno was fast losing his effervescence as the proud best man as he realised that the English worms he had ploughed into the bitter dust of oblivion had now resurfaced and grown sharp teeth.

I called to the photographer, 'Ça va?'

He was indeed very happy and gave us the thumbs up indicating that our impromptu appearance was captured for his client's posterity.

I wonder if he captured the even more interesting developments that were about to occur. My devious little brain had finally alighted on one very appropriate punishment for his crime. I had espied with my little eye something beginning with S.

S stands for Swimming Pool, which I could see rippling tantalizingly through reception's plate glass wall.

'Jumbo! Come here, now! Lads, let's get the bastard.'

I dived at Eno's feet and upended him. At first, the wedding guests laughed as they all knew me as The Clown in France and thought I was providing them with a little free entertainment. Then when Jumbo arrived, he and my brother Pete took Eno's two flailing arms and we marched him horizontally outside to the beckoning pool. With great joy in my heart I was thinking, today we are to give new meaning to the phrase 'Frog March'...

Sensing the wet punishment that loomed every step closer, the slippery toad began to scream, shout and beg for mercy.

Showing no mercy, the Captain of the Good Ship Revenge screamed, 'Hear me now lads. A frog belongs in the water doesn't it?'

'Aye, Cap'n', rejoined my jolly shipmates.

'Heave ho, me lads!'

One...Two...Three...

Lads, Eno's away...

Everything was in glorious slow motion, each frame recorded on the 38mm Panavision of my mind. I had cherished this desire to meet and greet Eno for a whole year and now my brain, eager to taste and savour this historic moment for eternity had slowed its whole fortuitous execution down into separate frame by frame milli-seconds, allowing me to relish the desperate look, as he took flight with a *Sacre Bleu!* etched on his cheating-agent's face.

His unceremonious dunking gave us all boundless feelings of pleasure as his immaculate mohair suit and shiny Rolex watch were consigned to the same fate as the toad they so submissively adorned. I said to the Rolex and the mohair that if you lie down with dogs then you are bound to get fleas, so the chlorinated pool is the best place for all of you right now.

The wedding guests didn't know what to make of it and after depositing a number of high profile English expletives into the pool to keep him company, we left for our rooms to take sweet rest, laughing like kids all the way.

We had lost everything over that period due to his treachery, but suddenly as we lay upon our soft beds we were rich men again, every one of us.

You can see that as a spiritual aspirant I have still a long way to go to considering myself the finished article, because, sorry to say, even as I am writing this, I am still chuckling about the sweet mischief of that day.

After being mauled and mobbed in concerts and public appearances all over Britain, I was stressed, disenchanted, and I wanted out. At that point, conveniently enough, a large jovial man named Roy Farrant had turned up.

Roy had been a roadie for the sixties band The Tremeloes. He offered to take the strain of dealing with it all. He talked me out of leaving and took the pressure off. Thanks to him I was able to stay a Rubette for a bit longer.

During that time I saw exactly what money did to people, what booze did too, and above all, what people did to people. I always had the idealistic notion that, if I ever became famous and had all I had ever wished for, life as a whole, give or take the occasional hiccup, would be sorted. A couple of kids, a couple of cars, a house on the hill, then it would all be great. Well, in a couple of years I had all those things, plus a swimming pool and grassed tennis court. And guess what? I wasn't happy at all.

Something was missing inside me. I felt an emptiness that nothing could fill. Money didn't fill it. Performing didn't fill it. The adulation of thousands of fans didn't fill it.

More and more, while I was on the road, I started to read from the Gideon's Bible. Each hotel we stayed in had a copy in a drawer somewhere and I drew a lot of solace from it. While it didn't answer all the questions that my anxious heart and mind constantly threw up, it had so many beautiful and wonderful things in it, that I decided it was time to lean further towards the direction of spirituality.

The guys thought this was hilarious. I would enthuse about bits and pieces I had read, and try to get the others to share my enthusiasm, or at least listen. After a while, I could see that they were not very pleased with me. In fact I was driving them nuts.

But as time ran on and we were touring further and further afield, my interest in spiritual things deepened, and I eventually decided that my true path in life was going to be a spiritual one.

Nine

THE TURNING POINT CAME for me after a gig in Manchester. We arrived drunk back at Mickey's house around three in the afternoon. Mickey got out and his wife Val apparently rang Cherrille to say I was two minutes away.

Slouched in the back of our stretch limo, stinking of excess from the night before, I was driven round the corner from Ecclestone Crescent to Ilfracombe Gardens. There I saw a sight that impacted strongly on my heart: the figures of three people who loved me more than anything or anyone else in the world.

My wife had got the children nicely dressed. The three of them looked radiant and loving, excited about welcoming their hero back into their arms after his long tour.

This fraction of a second contained within it the sacred moment which turned my life around.

I could not be one person when I was away and someone else at home. It was time to be true to myself and to them. I had had enough. I had achieved what I thought I had always yearned for materially, but it had not fulfilled me. At that moment I knew it would not be long before I would have nothing to do with the life that until then had meant so much to me.

Following on from that I began to study many religious and spiritual beliefs, and tried following different paths. I wanted to find if there really was a God. Was he the Christian God? The Jewish God? The Hindu God?

Confused by it all, not knowing where to start, I decided that whoever God was, I was sure He, She or It would be happy if I served God's children even if I didn't know who their Mother or Father was. I was confident that the answer would come when I was ready for it and not a moment before.

The balmy summer of 1976 saw us all relocated to posh detached houses in salubrious tree-lined districts. While the other lads were avidly pursuing affluent lifestyles, full of new cars, holidays and gadgets, and Alan was in the throes of purchasing a twin-engined plane, I was looking for something else.

To satisfy my growing interest in an alternative lifestyle, I held a weekly open night at my house in Gidea Park where I invited learned spiritual communicators and skilful healers to give demonstrations. But watching others was not enough; I wanted with all my heart and soul to do this work myself.

Cherrille never complained about my switch in direction and allegiances. She neither hated nor loved what we had or what we were. Although far from a fool, she was simple in her life and her tastes. Occasionally she might go out and have a little spend-up, but essentially she only liked money because having it meant she didn't have to worry about not having it as previously.

After several years of dabbling, I decided to get some qualifications in the healing arts, which would eventually lead to me having a clinic at home and then a health shop and clinic in nearby Romford.

I took a six-month course in remedial massage and underwent training in reflexology. Within a couple of years I had a working knowledge of herbal medicine and Bach Flower remedies. Funnily enough, the Northern Institute of Massage, where I studied remedial massage, held their weekend massage courses in Cleethorpes at a hotel next door to the place where The Rubettes had their first gig five years earlier.

In 1979 we met Terry Edwards. He was a scientist and spiritualist, who encouraged us to become vegetarians. This was the only time that Cherrille resisted my changes. She worried that dissonance around the dining table would threaten our sweet family relationship.

I promised Cherrille I would eat everything the family ate except the meat. Pia backed me and became a semi-veggie, still having fish for some time. Cherrille and Scott continued on as before. When Cherrille realised that there was no danger of the family unit being rent asunder, she and our son joined me and Pia a couple of years later.

I opened up the east wing of our mock Tudor mansion in Gidea Park as a healing sanctuary with a restful waterfall. I bought a massive quadraphonic sound system from Elton John – he had been given it while he was touring Japan, and had no use for it, so I snapped it up. I used it to play soothing New Age music to my patients.

Two members of The Rubettes had departed over the preceding years to do their own thing without too much negative effect on the band. We were now down to four: Alan, Mickey, Tony and me, and our latest records were reaching lower positions than our earlier hits. We were at a crossroads.

Our recording contract with State Records was close to expiring, and at this rate we would get peanuts if we signed a new one with them. Then Wayne and Tony served us up a song entitled *Foe Dee Oh Dee*.

Oh dee indeed. When we walked into the recording studio in Chipping Norton Oxford to cut the disc, I nearly fainted when I saw the lyrics planted tauntingly on the music stand. It should have been entitled Ticket To Obscurity.

I was always grateful for the chance at fame and riches that Wayne and Tony had placed before us, and rightly so. After the first massive hit it was morally incumbent upon us to have them continue writing and guiding our musical direction. The other big hits - *Juke Box Jive*, *I Can Do It* and *Tonight* - were worthy pieces of writing and production. But not this.

'This is genocide on your part and suicide on ours,' I said passionately to Wayne. He was having none of it. We could all write, but Wayne had not allowed it and had tied us down to B sides only.

I recalled a night early on in our partnership when Wayne invited us all to an exclusive West End restaurant. He reserved a VIP room for the proceedings and then began to wine and dine us to the point of nigh extinction. Soon we all closely resembled inebriated putty in his hand.

'By the way lads, there are a few things we should sort out for the future success of us all, individually and conjointly.' Wayne struck the perfect balance between friendliness and authority.

'Tony and I will write all of the music in the future, both A and B sides, as well as all the albums.'

You could have heard a pin drop. Each one of us looked at the other, not knowing what to do or what to say. We were all frustrated writers, but Wayne after all was like an angel to us – he had fed and richly clothed our families, he had also put the expensive roofs of our expensive houses over our expensive heads. But this?

The silence lingered.

'Good then. I will take that as an okay.'

'No, Wayne!' I cried, sounding like Oliver Twist asking for more. 'That's not fair.'

Wayne struggled to hold back his annoyance.

'That's the way I see it, lads.'

'Here's the way I see it,' I said, suddenly sober. 'We're very grateful for what we've been given, but we're writers too, and we want a chance to shape and mould our own destiny. To that end, we'll write all our B sides and half the albums.'

The boys still never said a word.

Even though we owed much to Wayne and Tony, *Sugar Baby Love* didn't make it to the top fifty until we gave it that spectacular nudge on Top of the Pops. We had a part in its success and should be rewarded proportionately.

Wayne caved in, knowing that he and Tony needed us as much as we needed them. The boys returned from their silent exile and began to chat animatedly. I felt the relief of one who has lanced a Vesuvius of a boil.

Contractual arrangements were duly made and everyone was happy – until this awful record.

I knew we must have the right to protect ourselves from the totalitarian rule when that rule became opposed to our mutual successes. And it had. *Foe Dee Oh Dee* barely scraped into the Top 30. Despite the fact we had created a wonderful track around it, you can't polish a turd.

Well, we wouldn't be visiting any more VIP lounges after this effort.

Before we arrived at our contract's end, due to my vituperative nature, I was allowed to write our last single, *Baby I Know*. Despite reservations from both Wayne and State Records it was released and KA POW, it zoomed into the Top Ten. Twenty places higher than Wayne's *Foe Dee Oh Dee*.

Now we were in a much more advantageous position. It came the very week our contract with Wayne's label, State Records, terminated. Our manager Big Roy strolled cockily into Polydor records on the day *Baby I Know* had sold twenty thousand copies. Nowadays twenty thousand copies will put you at number one in the chart. We once sold that in a day.

After an hour's negotiation, Roy walked out with £750,000 in advance royalties. Suddenly, the music world was a wonderful place to be associated with again.

Alas, horror of horrors, we got cocky. If pride cometh before a fall, how we plummeted. *Baby I Know* had a country flavour to it, quite a departure from our usual, quasi rock-n-roll cuts that preceded it. We wanted to break into the album market, trying to emulate the Eagles, so I penned and sang the next release, *Ladies of Laredo*, which was very slow and, at eight minutes, too long, too slow and shall we say in hindsight a tad indulgent. It was too long for plays, too slow for radio, and in short, too cool for school.

Sour grapes aside, I had actually become more interested in following my spiritual path anyway. So, shortly after, my destiny began to unfold in that tantalising direction.

Part Two
Never Say Die

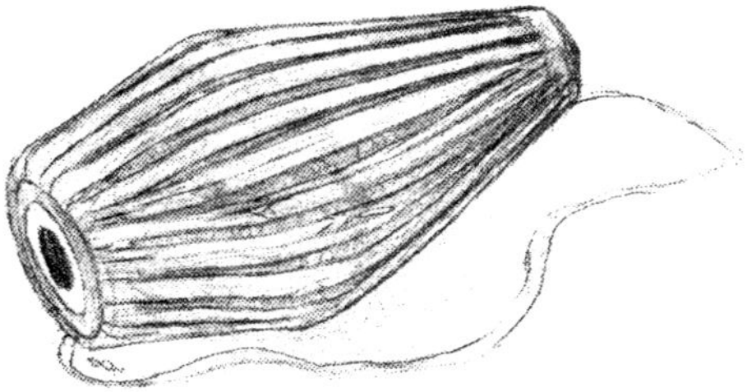

Ten

I KNEW THAT TO GET KNOWN as a complementary healer I would have to do things for free for quite some time: help neighbours, friends, anybody who needed it. But I was ready, willing and able. They say that when the student is ready, the teacher will appear. My teacher was Terry Edwards.

He taught me some techniques of spiritual healing and also talked to me about my clairvoyant abilities and how best to develop them. He was a scientist and a very brilliant person. We became friends.

It was in 1980 or thereabouts when I began to realise that my best friends were now becoming people from the healing arts instead of the performing arts, and our open house policy was attracting a number of interesting personalities into our fast changing lives. We opened up our home to any sincere soul who had something to offer. We were introduced to Karl Francis who could read and interpret the aura. He explained that the aura is a subtle electromagnetic field around the body, made of the mind's intelligence and ego, amongst other things. Karl was also a Kabbalist, a mystic process with roots in Judaism. We also invited such characters as Clive James, a psychic artist who could draw spirit guides, departed loved ones and angels, and Marie Cherie, a Scottish clairvoyant who was popular around that time.

By 1981, I had opened up a health shop in Albert Road,

Romford and I was doing reflexology, massage and herbal remedies. There were about three hundred herbal mixtures and potions that I was making up for people, as well as Bach Flower Remedies.

Helen Perfect, our next door neighbour, was my business partner and between us we put the whole thing together. Bob, her friendly husband, showed me how to put up a shelf and a cupboard and left me to screw and bang for a week until we had the semblance of a health shop. Our holistic little creation, which Helen naturally named Perfect Health, was soon stocked with lots of healthy whole foods, exotic herbal teas, vegetarian 'meat' products... In short, pretty much all the things that we adored and the local populace of Romford were absolutely willing to live without. Unsurprisingly, we suffered financially pretty much the entire time we were in business, so I had to start playing in pubs again in the evenings to supplement our income. We did better on the healing front, though. I seemed to have a knack with people, finding the right herbs, diets and therapies. I made quite a name for myself. Years later I was officially recognised when a grateful client named Suzanne secretly contacted my other patients and prompted them all to write in to the *Journal for Alternative and Complimentary Medicine* who were holding a nationwide competition for the country's best healers.)

I served in the shop four days a week, and for two I treated folk in the clinic. Dear Cherrille followed me into my new adventure and worked in the shop too, but got extremely bored as she found herself sitting waiting sometimes for hours between customers.

We were still living at this time in the massive rambling millionaire's mansion. I was, however, earning less than £100 a week and savings were dwindling rather sharpish. We had our lovely Pia and Scott to take care of, so I began to give the whole subject of good economics some hard thought and decided that eventually we might have to downgrade our home so I could afford to continue on my path as a seeker of the truth. My wife, bless her heart, was four square behind me on it, too.

Peter Ashley, one of Terry's connections who lived out in the wilds of Felixstowe, came to offer his skills. Peter was a self-possessed person, confident and personable. He claimed that he could take people back to past lives; and one night in our lounge he proceeded to hypnotize everybody in the room. Everybody except me. I wasn't keen. I didn't have the confidence in him that he obviously had in himself. After hypnotizing everyone in the room, he brought them back to the present and invited them to share any interesting experiences they may have had.

Though some of the stories were intriguing, I wasn't fully convinced past life regressions were genuine.

I had, however, had some psychic experiences of life beyond death. In 1979, five years after the Rubettes initial sucess, I went to see a succinct and magnificent demonstration by Ronald Beesley of reading and interpreting the aura. When the demonstration was over, I knew I had to study with him as soon as I had time in my busy touring schedule, and I found some precious time, too. Unfortunately, Mr Beesley was killed in a coach crash in India several days before we were to meet. I attended the course run by his dedicated followers.

Nearing the end of the week long course, during one deep meditation, Mr Beesley came to me. Dressed in a kilt and a feathered stalker's cap, he danced merrily up and down, saying emphatically, 'Get them all to do Knees up Mother Brown for God's sake. Liven things up please; this misery is not what my life was about.' Of course he referred to the cloud of gloom that naturally hung over his centre on the beach there in Pevensey Bay, Sussex, due to his untimely departure.

After we had all awakened, I reluctantly approached Cicely, Mr Beesley's right hand lady, a great soul in her own right, and told her exactly what I had seen and heard. To my amazement, she took me into her arms and warmly hugged me.

'You've definitely met Mr Beesley!' she beamed. 'He had a kilt and a feathered stalker's cap, just as you said, and whenever he wanted to lift our spirits, he would do a Knees up Mother Brown dance for us. You are *soooo* correct young man. Well done!'

The day after meeting Peter and observing the techniques that he had employed to regress folk, I had an early morning appointment with Irene, a young lady in her mid-twenties who was suffering from Multiple Sclerosis. Some months previously she had started to attend weekly massage and reflexology sessions with me at the shop and as I was pressing different parts of her feet my mind began to wander over events the of the previous night. My mind was still boggling when something urged me to say, 'Irene, you know massage and reflexology is not going to cure you. I think you have a shock or a trauma deep within, and that is what I believe is causing your physical condition. I'm sure it's coming from a shock.' Sometimes I would come out with stuff like that and I didn't even know where it came from. Maybe it was that same voice that comforted me at the loss of our baby.

'What do you mean?' she asked, forcing me to gather my senses again.

'Did your first husband beat you?'

'No.'

'Any upsets? Traumas? Anxiety?'

'No.'

'Was your birth okay?'

'Yes, it was fine.'

'It must be from a past life, then.'

'Past life? Are you mad?'

'No. I'll show you if you like. Would you be prepared to take a chance?'

'I s'pose so,' replied Irene.

I copied what Peter had done only the day before. I guess I needed to know for myself if the technique he had utilised was genuine or not. Next thing I know, the cowboy that I am, I was putting Irene into a trance. No training, no experience, just this blind urge inside to do it. Irene was a wonderful trance subject and effortlessly slipped back to the time where the issues around her condition lay lodged within the deep recesses of her subconscious.

She was once a Native American. She described fascinating aspects of her life, how she lived, what took place in her encampment. I was riveted by what she was saying. She said that one day the men left the encampment on a hunting trip. In their absence another tribe came, raped the women, including her, and then put half a dozen arrows in her solar plexus before departing.

I was amazed at this, but then I realised that I was supposed to be helping this person forget her trauma, not make her re-live the experience lying on the ground, dying. I had a good idea of what took place at time of death through my associations with Terry Edwards my psychic friend. I knew that the subtle body would leave, carrying the imprint of that life through into her next life, and her whole physical and mental future would be determined at that time, by that imprint. So I said, 'Just float out of the body.' Then, more gently, I said, 'Now leave it all behind. Can you see your body down there on the ground?'

'Yes, yes, I can,' she said. She was very disturbed.

'All this shock, all this terror, all this horror, I want you to deposit it all back into that body you're looking at now because you don't need that body any more. Take a deep breath. You can feel, Irene. You are alive. And you are well. Free from the pain, fear and trauma.'

Little by little, I encouraged her to disassociate herself from that bloodied lump of flesh and any trauma connected to it.

The gentle smile that began to warm and loosen her taut face convinced me that the shock had been dumped back into her slain physical body that was now lying on history's floor. A few deep breaths and the trauma was gone. I brought her back to waking consciousness.

She was very shaken. So was I come to that. I didn't tell her it was my first time. She went out a little dazed but not disturbed.

'Thanks, I'll see you next week,' was all she said.

She'd been seeing me every week for several months but when the next week came, she missed her appointment. She didn't call. She didn't turn up the week after that, either. A long time passed.

I was too scared to call her. About three months later I saw her father, a very grim-looking but quiet man. This day he stood outside our little health shop, staring, with a thick white envelope in his hand. I thought the worst and immediately panicked.

He came inside and walked straight up to me, thrust the envelope into my hand and said, 'Don't try to give it back or there will be trouble.' And then he left.

What did he mean trouble? What has he done? What have I done? I tried to get my wife to open it but she wouldn't. So I went into the back room, about to faint at the fact that my whole career was over now. I'd worked and studied literally day and night to get some qualification and run this shop and now, after all this struggle, I'd ruined it all by doing something without qualification - probably maimed someone as well. 1981 was set to be the year of my renaissance. Instead I feared it had become the year of the twit.

I opened the envelope.

> Dear John,
>
> Thank you so much for what you did for Irene. Since you did that, the use of her leg and her arm have come back and she has been to the hospital but they cannot find any trace of the MS. Thank you very much.

And there was 100 pounds in crisp, five pound notes. I had to sit down before I fell down – the relief for Irene and for my career was tremendous. And I had 100 smackers to boot!

I would often be challenged on this particular story in the mid to late eighties, when I gave lectures in some of the UK's prominent seats of learning, including Cambridge, Imperial College London, LSE, Kings, Brunel, to name a few. The point was mentioned that MS can sometimes go into remission for some time. But this is not the only possible explanation.

At that time there were several reincarnation hypnotherapists in the country, but none, at least that I had heard of, who were curing mental or physical disorders in the process. I wasn't prepared to look any deeper at that time because it was such a shock for me. Not being trained in that area, I decided to give that very specialized experience a wide berth for a while and concentrated more on the physical than the subtle soul. (I am please to say that, thirty years later, Irene still has had no recurrence of her illness.)

Peter Ashley had, however, lit a small but glowing fire in my life with what I had learned from him that night in the early eighties. That fire was to eventually blaze and illumine the path to my destiny.

When I took to spiritual life Helen, due to her love for us, was ready to keep an open mind about what we were getting into. Bob her husband, however, was critical of anything that smacked of religion and although he tried to tolerate my almost 180 degree life swerve it did drive a wedge between us. Helen was working full time in the shop with me and was witnessing some of the wonderful healings that the Upstairs Management was awarding us and indeed had her own superb experiences with past life regression. In previous lives, she'd been locked up in Newgate Prison for a slight misdemeanour, died under an upturned sled in Scandanavia, and in another been a honey bee drunk from flower nectar through performing the floral equivalent of an East End pub crawl.

One Autumn night there came a rat-tat-tat on the front door. An old Indian gentleman was standing there.

'I understand that you're looking for God,' he said.

'Excuse me, but who are you?' I asked.

'I am Mr Sharma, a retired schoolmaster from Agra in India and I am living next door to you with my son Dr Sharma.'

'Oh, do come in,' I returned, rather redundantly as he was already half-way down the reception hall. I showed him to my healing room in the east side of the house and offered the venerable old gent a comfortable seat on the 1930s settee. He looked very at home among the Art Deco fine furnishings that I had collected on my travels and I imagined that when he was a young man he probably sat in chairs and decor like this, rather gravely marking the Hindi and Sanskrit papers of his pupils.

'What are your interests?' he asked rather purposefully.

I couldn't wait to tell him how much I knew and how good I was at helping people. At the end of my long soliloquy he said calmly, 'So what do you know about Rama and Krishna?'

'Not a lot. I've seen those nutty Hare Krishnas on the streets and I've got one of their books somewhere.'

'Oh, very good,' he said.

'What do you know about Rama and Krishna, Mr

Sharma?'

The spiritual floodgates then duly opened. An hour sailed effortlessly, painlessly, fascinatingly by into the next hour and beyond. At his explanation's closure I can only say I was mesmerized by the magic of his presentation. My heart proclaimed, 'This Is It!' I'd never felt so happy, so satisfied. I didn't know it then, but this old man from the other side of the world was to become my first guru.

Before he left, I introduced him to my wife who, although polite, had some small misgivings about him that she couldn't quite put her finger on. Whatever he was or wasn't, I loved his company and his deep enthusiasm to share his knowledge of God. He was also a father type figure.

I didn't enjoy such a convivial relationship with my own Dad and over some lengthy periods of time he was out of my life and out of the children's life as well. Then one day I heard he was in a wheelchair due to his rheumatism and arthritis, and I decided to forgive the past. Life is too short. I used my massage skills and my knowledge of herbal remedies and before long, my father had been put back together again. To his credit, he was very grateful for my assistance, but in general I kept a healthy distance between us most of the time.

Eleven

MANY THINGS CHANGED after Mr Sharma came knock-knocking. Due to his benign influence, I started to chant a mantra that he had given me as part of my spiritual practices. Then, after three months, in what I now understand to be an initiation ceremony, he made 'disciples' of a number of my family members who were unwittingly initiated. There was no stopping this dogged octogenarian who in a fit of missionary zeal 'initiated' not only family members, but a few innocent friends who happened to be passing by on the day. We had a fire ceremony at his behest, with smoke billowing around the room and Bob's dogs and our son Scott coughing away like good-uns, as unintelligible mantras filled the pungent air. Those words seemed like they could burn searing holes in our bad karma and magically transform our lives. My wife wasn't best pleased with our new 'guru' as one thing he'd definitely done was to burn a searing hole in our carpet in his zeal to give us Eastenders a taste of the Far East.

Mr Sharma was dressed in dhoti (traditional Indian wrap-around bottoms) with a tweed Nehru hat perched at a jaunty angle upon his shaved head. He threw copious amounts of grains into the flames pouring libations of ghee, or clarified butter, on top of them making them dance higher and higher. From time to time he would glance at this stout redoubtable Sanskrit verse book at his side.

Would we ever be the same after it was all over? I wasn't sure. I knew that the carpet wouldn't be, judging by the smell of scorched fabric assailing my nostrils

I was then re-named Krishna Rao and Cherrille was re-named Rukmini. All the kids and friends got new exotic names and it certainly seemed like our lives would be changed forever.

As well as chanting his mantra, for ten minutes each day I was also chanting the Hare Krishna Mantra that I got from a book called *Science of Self Realization.* A mantra is a sacred sound vibration that brings peace and well-being to the chanter. *Man* means mind and *Tra* means freeing. It literally frees the mind.

I had been a vegetarian for a couple of years due to the gentle influence of Terry Edwards, and I was putting more and more emphasis on my spiritual life; thus chanting mantras fitted in nicely for me at the time.

Looking back, I remember that early one morning, before all this had happened, Terry and I went for a walk along a cliff path after the Ronald Beesley seminar. Terry revealed to me a dream he'd had of how we were selling the group's equipment and that basically I was moving away from that world onto the true path I had been born to tread – devotional service to God and his children. We were still doing quite well as a group and though things were on the wane in England, we were still a force to contend within Europe, and specially in France.

I was glad to hear his dream prophecy; it felt both natural and exciting. I decided I needed to commit to a spiritual path. Shortly after I prayed to the Lord. My dear Lord, I prayed, if you want me to become a Christian that would be very nice, but I am not completely convinced at this time because of what I have read in the Bible, there are some things that are so beautiful and other things I don't quite understand. So you, being the Lord of everything and everyone's heart and everywhere, could you please kindly arrange for me to meet with a nice person who can fully explain your words and I will feel very glad to become your servant in this way.

It was a couple of days later, after we had returned home spiritually charged, there came that fateful knock on the door. And there stood Mr Sharma. He loved Rama, the sixth incarnation of Vishnu, the Maintainer in the Hindu Trinity of the Creator, Maintainer and Destroyer. The ancient Vedic literatures state that Lord Vishnu appeared on this Earth in the Silver Age as Rama, to demonstrate how a pious king should act. Just as Buddha, who is considered the ninth incarnation of Vishnu, taught *ahimsa* – non violence and worldly detachment – so Rama, taught by example how the ruling class should conduct themselves for the benefit of every living entity in society. The book of his life is called the *Ramayana*.

It was such a beautiful book and Mr Sharma completely transformed into a child when he read it. Sometimes laughing, sometimes becoming pensive and silent in between utterances and on the rare occasions, crying at the beauty contained in the verses. This was the kind of religion I'd been looking for. It was another one of those pivotal moments in my life.

Mr Sharma taught Cherrille how to cook some specialist foods. He even had me purchase a large stone from Green Lanes Indian shopping centre that he would sit patiently on the floor beside and rub various exotic looking foodstuffs against, creating fresh stone ground spices for cooking. He was always in and out of our house. When our friends called by, it was amusing for us to watch their shocked faces as Mr Sharma sat rub-rubbing in the corner on his stone, hardly looking up, while we pretended not to know he was there and continued our conversation seemingly unconscious of the aged Hindu slave we were holding captive in our kitchen.

At the time there were not as many vegetarian foodstuffs

available as there are now, so these developments in our culinary repertoire were very welcome treats. Things progressed quite smoothly, with either me popping into his house or he visiting us on a daily basis.

On one of my visits Mr Sharma asked me to open up one of his old, beaten, tin suitcases and carefully take out an even older looking pile of newspapers. I was expecting ancient scriptures, but instead I was greeted with some yellowed copies of a newspaper (I think it may have been the *Southampton Chronicle*) dated around the second decade of the 20th century.

I couldn't work out why Mr Sharma would be carrying around such a mundane publication within his sacred scripture boxes. He took the papers from me and opened them carefully at the page where he proudly read out an account written by Major Farrell of the Southampton Regiment.

The story went something like this: Major Farrell was stationed in India prior to the First World War. He was fascinated by Indian culture and was very happy to be posted there along with his wife. One day, whilst looking through his field glasses at the surrounding area of his encampment, he noticed through the rising heat haze that seemed to gently move the arid valley beyond, an old man with a very long grey beard. He was slowly walking by the bank of a sleepy river and appeared to be watching something in the water. He stopped walking, waded into the river and pulled out something that resembled a human form. It is customary in India that bodies are sometimes consigned to holy rivers like Ganges and Yamuna. The old man then dragged the body behind an ancient banyan tree and a little while later, a young man appeared from behind that tree and walked away.

Major Farrell ordered two of his men to apprehend that man. Twenty minutes later they appeared in the Major's tent with the young man. The commander told him that he had seen his strange actions and demanded to know what he was doing and where the old man had gone.

'I am the old man,' came the reply. He explained that he was a yogi who could 'vacate' his body when it got too old and worn-out. He did this by finding a corpse that was still 'fresh' and entering it. This vehicle would then be used until it too became too old and decrepit. He said he had been doing this for hundreds of years.

Major Farrell was so enthusiastic about sharing his experience that he asked the publisher to print his home address for anyone interested to know more.

It is said that yogis attain these mystic *siddhis* (supernatural powers) by adhering strictly to the *astanga* yoga system which is a very taxing regime of austerities involving drilling the respiration, *asanas* which are postures that have to be maintained for protracted periods of time, meditation, mantras, prayers and fasts; very difficult for the ordinary man.

In the same article the Major spoke of being called back to England to lead his regiment in the First World War. He said how he reluctantly left India and his dear wife to fight against the Germans in France. His article told that he had to lead his men over flat terrain to knock out a German machine gun post.

Once they had jumped out of their trenches to attack there was absolutely nowhere to shelter. It was do or die. Due to the odds being so stacked against them, it was more die than do as the unprotected soldiers were relentlessly mown down as they ran toward their adversary. The commander had only his pistol and his valour as his protection. With his head tucked in low he just kept running in the direction of the machine gun post as it continued to spew out instant death for hundreds of his men.

Halfway across the field he began to wonder, as from the

corners of both his eyes he could see the men either side of him dropping like flies, why he himself had somehow remained unharmed. To his utter amazement he looked up and saw a huge, long-haired figure clad in leopard skin, carrying in one hand a trident and screaming at the enemy with a blood curdling ferocious voice. Though thousands of bullets were striking his formidable form, they were simply bouncing off. He then disappeared as suddenly as he had appeared and by that time the unharmed major was able to take out the machine gun post.

When arriving back in India he was joyously re-united with his wife and after some time he shared with her this miraculous story. What she had to say brought great joy to my heart as it surely did to theirs. Mrs Farrell herself had been the cause of her husband's deliverance. Little could she have known that her prayers would be answered so graphically and dramatically.

Here's Mrs Farrell's version of the tale: When her husband left India, she feared she might never see him again. One day, head in hands, overcome with anxiety for her beloved husband, she heard a chorus of girls singing and chanting. She looked up and saw some brightly dressed young women in beautiful colourful saris, bearing fruits, cloth and various ornaments as though they were on their way to a party or a festival. Intrigued, she approached them, and with the little Hindi she knew, she asked where they were going.

'We're going to worship Lord Shiva. Would you like to come?'

Something within urged her to go too. In a few short minutes they all arrived at a temple of Lord Shiva, the Destroyer, where the girls offered their prayers and gifts in great joy. Before they departed, she thought that she should also say a prayer to Lord Shiva for her husband's safe return.

The Major listened spellbound. When she had finished he

asked, 'My dear, what did Lord Shiva look like at the temple?'

'He had long, matted locks and wore a leopard skin. He also carried a silver trident at his side.'

I was eager to spread the word on the amazing things I was learning. Whenever I had the opportunity to speak on esoteric matters I would do so, especially at the shop. Some 'customers' were just as keen to have me follow their doctrines too. Often they would come in to the shop on the pretext of making a purchase and bombard me with their uncomfortable type of hell-fire and damnation, then disappear without buying a blinking thing.

They'd caringly ask about my life and just when my heart was open they'd look piercingly into my eyes and pronounce:

'Have you surrendered your life unto Lord Jesus? If not, why not?'

My ample reasons often fell on deaf ears. So it was always an unproductive process, but I guess it helped me to understand deeply where my commitments really were and why I held them dear to my heart.

At first when I began to experience this evangelical drubbing of the psychic phenomena, I was loathe to respond strongly due to my love and respect of Lord Jesus. But as I became more and more exposed to that one-eyed zeal I began to respond likewise. My beliefs embraced, among other things, two vital philosophies: vegetarianism and reincarnation, which they summarily dismissed as the Devil's work. One fanatic even came with a coloured poster displaying a bowl of fruit and vegetables with red horns peering out from it, and the words 'The Devil's Food.'

So it was an interesting and challenging time. It seemed that the Devil got the blame/acclaim for too much in these processes. See how he's even awarded with a capital D? Since Reincarnation and Karma were removed from the Christian tenet – around the time of Emperor Constantine – more and more blame was apportioned to the devil than he rightly deserved. So instead of the good and bad served up for us in this life being directly a proportionate response to the good and bad dealt out by us previously, this devil/hell mode of belief abounds and confounds the simple truth that what goes around comes around. However, many of us may be too sentimentally charged to accept such simplicity.

Mr. Sharma was teaching us all to read Sanskrit and the *Ramayana*. I was happy to be progressing, however slowly, on this path. I decided once and for all to get away from show business. We sold the Gidea Park house in 1981 and bought a smaller house in a leafy grove in Hornchurch, sans mortgage – I knew I wouldn't be earning money. I would be earning perhaps enough to pay the ground rental, the rates, and everyday expenses but, from that time on I knew life had to be very simple.

I left the Rubettes and started full time at the shop. In 1984 the clinic struggled and finances stretched to the point beyond manageability. I had to respond to the calling of the East End pub circuit again as it began to call out in it's smoky gravelled voice for it's errant son to return. For the next five painful but solvent years I found myself once again slugging it out on the circuit in not very salubrious surroundings. Although the musos were always capable, friendly and accommodating they weren't the great musicians I had grown used to. In professional life I had been spoiled and thus it was quite a test for me.

I thought that in four to five months I could build my practice up and then I wouldn't have to do this stuff any more. But five long years later I was still playing in pubs. Then by some miracle a few philanthropic people - Colin Wilcox, Malcolm Stern and Roger Gewolb - decided for some very much appreciated reason to step in financially when they learned on the grapevine of my predicament. Malcolm is now well known in psychotherapy and counselling and has appeared in his own television series. Colin later became a multi-millionaire with his New Age label, New World Music. They were involved in tithing – giving 10% of their income to a worthy spiritual cause or person, which is supposed to bring back a good return, so to speak, financially as well as spiritually. So they gave me some money to write more spiritual pieces, which meant I could forsake all those smoky, poky pubs.

I was finally able to indulge myself in spiritual studies and write spiritual songs.

But what to write?

Twelve

HELEN AND I WERE ATTENDING a bring and buy sale in Ongar, when Helen purchased a copy of the *Bhagavad Gita* - the sacred Vedic text which first taught me about reincarnation - for 10 pence and excitedly brought it back to me at our stall.

Terry Edwards often quoted the book when he gave philosophical talks at Laindon Spiritualist Church, so I was grateful to receive and study it further.

In amongst the dozens of philosophical/spiritual and New Age books that I was surrounding myself with, I found a 5000 year old text named *Bhagavad Gita*. I was to discover later that great philosophers and writers like Thoreau, Gandhi and Emerson regarded it as one of the most illuminating discourses on self-realization ever written. Still to this day it continues to provide me with insight into the amazing nature of each one of us.

The *Bhagavad Gita* is spoken by Krishna who consoles his friend Arjuna with the knowledge that the soul, the self, is eternal, and the body is a temporary thing. At death, the soul, along with all the impressions and actions from its previous existence, goes on to a fresh body and receives the karma appropriate to its previous deeds. The *Gita* says:

> As a person takes off old garments and puts on new ones,

similarly the soul sheds the physical overcoat of the body and puts on the new one.

Reading the *Gita* opened up a new world of wonder and beauty that no book to date has emulated. For some unknown reason I decided to render the 10th and 11th chapters to music: The Universal Form and The Opulences of the Absolute, respectively.

In a couple of months I had created a nice pop opera and it was suggested that we put it on in St James's Church, Piccadilly. Malcolm, one of my sponsors, was the director there and helped arrange it. My daughter was going to play Arjuna, Krishna's friend, and my son was going to be the scribe, Sanjaya, who telepathically receives this whole conversation between Arjuna and Krishna, played by yours truly. We put it all together the best that untrained actors could.

We needed appropriate costumes. Where could we find such garments?

I'd seen Hare Krishnas in the streets when we were recording *Juke Box Jive* in Air Studios on Regent Street. They came twirling around the corner there, exuding ecstatic otherworldliness in their flowing saffron robes. Although something in my heart told me that their dancing and chanting was a profound activity, they didn't seem to connect with the common folk passing by, including me.

As time was getting perilously short before the performace of our pop opera, I reluctantly visited the Hare Krishna temple in Soho Street and spoke to the Temple president.

'I've got one of your books and I've written this music – '

'And you speculated the hell out of it, didn't you?' he cut me off before I could continue.

I had been right; I couldn't deal with these people. They were in another world. I came away a little dejected. It was only a couple of days before our opera and I still hadn't got any blinkin' costumes.

I reluctantly returned to the temple, but this time I was armed with a recording of the backing track and my little tape player. I hit the play button before he had a chance to say anything, and I began to sing.

I sang the whole 10th and 11th chapters off by heart and by the end of it he was moved to tears.

They ended up providing costumes, a meal for the audience, and lighting and video equipment to film the opera.

Little by little, I got to know the Krishna devotees. Mr Sharma, however, didn't like them much and, unfortunately, he and I had a falling out. He'd got a little carried away with some of the female disciples I had introduced him to from the shop. I prepared to accept an apology and explanation but, to my amazement, he was having none of it and never displayed a jot of contrition. So, as painlessly as possible, I sadly had to remove myself and my family from his influence. I took more and more shelter in the Krishna devotees and became familiar and comfortable with them. My wife, to my great surprise, was even more enthusiastic about our new friendship with the devotees than I was. She is generally very reticent about committing to anything without deep consideration, but she also weighs up people and things with unerring accuracy, as she had with Mr Sharma. One day we were to have a meeting with the Krishna people at their London headquarters when she said, 'This meeting is going to be a massive turning point in our life, you realise that, don't you?'

She never spoke like that. That was my style, not hers. I could see she was relishing the new life and the future that silently and yet forcibly seemed to beckon. It was indeed to be a massive turning point for us.

The night of our performance at St James Church in Piccadilly was soon upon us. We entered the beautiful church that Sir Christopher Wren had built, and there above the door, as bold as brass, were the words: 'Turning Point' presents The Bhagavad Gita by John Richardson.

Cherrille flipped me a knowing wink. It was a good sign.

The show was a great success, even though I missed a few words here and there. My son, Scott, was the real star of the show, turning in an impeccable, word-perfect performance.

Terry was not so sure about my growing involvement with the devotees. His strong belief was that the soul travelled only onward and upward from each successive birth till it gained perfection, which for him meant merging into the oneness of God; whereas the Krishna viewpoint said that the human birth could not be taken for granted, and misuse of it could degrade a person down into lower species of life. Furthermore, their idea of liberation was to be re-united with God in a personal way and render ecstatic loving service to him.

I must admit, I favoured Terry's view on reincarnation, as I could not see what would be learned in an animal's form. I liked the devotees very much; I liked the chanting – though I wasn't so keen on their dancing at that point – and I loved their food. I thought perhaps some of their information, being 5,000 years old, was a bit out of date.

Terry's spiritualism had been my first entry into exploring who we were and what we were here for. The Spiritualist movement, although shunned by the Christians and the Church in general, had its own differences. On one side we had the Christian Spiritualists, who believed in one life only and salvation through the Lord Jesus; on the other side were the Spiritualists who believed in reincarnation, which was Terry's affiliation.

As far as reincarnation was concerned, I accepted it as the axiomatic truth. As far as misuse of the human form condemning a soul to life in an animal's body, the jury was still out. Krishna philosophy also says that the process of reincarnation is set up by the dying person's last thoughts. Whatever state of being you remember at time of death that will be the soul's next destination.

I thought it was all getting a bit complicated. What's a boy to do? Does he walk away? Does he take a bit from this path and a bit from that path? Or does he give up and go down the pub?

I asked myself whether I truly believed that there is a God who is everywhere, knows everyone and everything. I wasn't totally sure of the answer. So I postulated. What would you do in such a predicament, remembering that if you sit on the fence too long you might get piles? I concluded that if a person really believed in the existence of such a Being, they should ask that Being to show them the truth. So, on behalf of the person I hoped one day I might become, I prayed for an answer and then let my thoughts rest. The ball was firmly planted in the 'Upstairs Management's' court and I could get on with the things in my life that were within my control.

After Irene's astonishing story about her Native American past, I decided to work more on physical ailments in my clinic and give the psycho/spiritual stuff a miss for the while. However, as I gave my clients massages they would talk to me as though I was an old friend. Somehow I would come up with answers and perspectives that would help them.

I helped one woman, Doris, stop smoking in one session but she returned for another, asking, 'What shall we do? I don't have the need to smoke any more.'

I'd been reading a lot and needed to find out more about this animal birth stuff. But was it even possible to communicate with an animal if a soul was regressed to one? I was about to find out.

'I want you to go back to any lifetime in any century you choose. You will communicate with me at all times in the English language.'

Doris was a deep trance subject and sailed effortlessly back through her own personal history. I asked what she was and what she could see.

'I'm a lovely black horse,' she boldly declared. She began telling me all about her life as a horse. If I took her back to the life directly before this and she was a lower animal, that would indicate that Terry might be right about the transcendent journey of the soul. I was sure that's what I was about to witness.

I took her back to the life directly before the horse... and blow me down! She was a girl living on a farm in Somerset during the Industrial Revolution. As she spoke, the lady's accent took a dramatic swing from Essex to a powerful West Country brogue.

It was the time that many of the farms were emptying and farmers were going to the Promised Land: cities whose streets were allegedly paved with gold. What really awaited them of course was another kind of hell. She became an upstairs-downstairs maid, which she loathed and got hopelessly stuck in that miserable labour for sixty long years before finally dying alone and miserable in an attic.

So how does a human end up taking birth as a horse in the very next life?

I took our parlour lady to the time of death. She was dying alone and unloved in the top floor bedroom of the house where she worked.

'As you prepare for the end, I would like you to tell me what exactly is going through your mind. I know you hated the work you've been doing for so long. Are you feeling frustrated or depressed?' I asked.

'No, not at all,' came the unanticipated reply. 'I feel happy to be leaving this prison. I'm happy. I'm thinking of the countryside where I was born and lived in the early part of my life. I'm thinking of those lovely black horses...'

I was stunned. Here was my proof. How could it be that a woman unread in any philosophical or spiritual literature, could furnish me with information that colluded with the timeless teachings of the Vedas?

These ancient writings are awash with statements warning us about how material attachment brings us back to this material world, time and time again.

As far as God was concerned, I thought, well that's fine for Him, sitting on His golden throne while we're left to sink or swim in this mess. Many passionate debates have raged back and forth on this subject and through them I have realised that it's not that a cruel God is punishing us by shoving us into an unfavourable body, it's purely our own consciousness that sends the soul here and there on its journey, seeking fulfilment, freedom and independence. Whatever kind of body one currently has was created by one's previous consciousness.

More specifically, the *Gita* says, 'Whatever state of being you remember at time of death, that state will you attain without fail.' So at the time prior to her demise her focus and attraction for 'them beautiful black horses' took her to that very life. Incidentally, she spent one birth as a horse then re-emerged in a human form again.

I had begun to truly consider that the friend the ancient teachings refer to as Supersoul, or the Lord in the Heart, might be the one who showed me my future as a drummer; the one who warned me of the machine guns in France; the one who consoled me when our babies died; and maybe had been with me for all eternity.

Thirteen

FIFTEEN-YEAR-OLD SHELLEY was the subject for one of the most outstanding regressions that I ever had the honour to participate in. In 1986, while visiting from the USA for the summer vacation, Shelley became fascinated by the stories told by our family members about our regression experiences and was eager to discover her own past lives. I usually only worked with adults, but she was very determined to read the earlier chapters of her history. After receiving permission from her parents, she put good-natured pressure on me until I caved in and within minutes of doing so, she had organised her appointment with me in the clinic at the bottom of the garden, that evening at 7 pm sharp.

When I arrived at my little clinic/recording studio just before sunset, she was already sitting on my treatment couch with her legs swinging happily over the side, face beaming in anticipation.

'Okay,' I said. 'Now listen carefully as I explain the procedure.' I continued and Shelley nodded or shook her head at the appropriate moments. She also asked lots of intelligent questions, demonstrating a very sharp intellect beyond her tender years.

Formalities over, I began the induction and found her to be a wonderful subject; able to effortlessly switch off the conscious mind and drift deep into the realms of the sub-conscious. Indeed, she was a hypnotherapist's dream, as she could very quickly enter into the most profoundly altered state.

In not more than 5 minutes, she was experiencing her last life as an Anglo-Indian girl, named Annabel Singh. She lived most of her young life in Bengal, but had paid one visit to England in the mid-sixties, staying in London for a short time. She also recounted a memorable trip to Bombay where she described a well-known Hindu temple called the Maha Laxmi Mandir with detail no one could have known without having been there.

Over the next six weeks during the summer of 1986 we took Shelley back into earlier and earlier chapters of her Book of Life, as we referred to it, with more and more fascinating results.

The session that took place around the 6th week was the most fascinating. We had been ploughing back incrementally and thoroughly so that we could monitor the evolution of one life to the next. Then during this particular session we found ourselves in the middle of the eighteenth century and we began the familiar routine of question and answer:

'Ok, so looking around you. Do you sense yourself to be inside or outside?' I ask.

'I'm inside the Emperor's Palace at Schonbrumm in Vienna.'

'Oh, do you live there?'

'No, of course not. I'm just here to play forte piano for the Emperor with Nannerl.'

'Who's Nannerl?'

'She's my sister.'

'So are you accomplished on the piano, I mean, are you good?'

'I'm the best in the world,' she replied, waggishly.

'Oh yeah, so how old are you?'

'I'm six.'

'Perhaps you could tell me your name?' I gently coaxed.

'Perhaps you could tell me yours?' came the surprising reply.

I'd never had that before; the subject relating in a very present way. Sometimes this can happen on the rare occasion that a ghost or another spirit is being hosted within the psyche of the client. The way that this can be tested is to move the client from that incarnation to another known life. If it is a ghost, it will refuse to leave the life we are dealing with and will want to remain in so-called pole position for as long as it is possible. I quickly moved Shelley from this life to Annabel Singh without the slightest trace of resistance or reluctance. Satisfied that this character was indeed hers and not some disembodied entity wanting to have some fun, I continued.

'My name's John, what's yours?'

'All right, my name is Wolfgang.'

I know precious little about 18th century music, but I sensed this personality was a very important historical character and so I did what I've never done before. I asked Shelley to open her eyes while still in trance and held a writing pad in front of her chest. Remembering she had said she was six years old, I quickly took her forward in time to when she was older. With her head lifted slightly so that she could see what she was doing, I put a biro in her hand and requested a signature.

I was aware that Shelley was left handed and was a little surprised when she began writing with her right hand, with a very unusual script, the names Wolfgang Amade Mozartt.

But it's not Amade, it's Amadeus, and Mozart is spelt with one t not two, I told myself. I concluded that everyone wants to be someone famous, and regarded the rest of the session with more than a little scepticism, although I did not project that on to Shelley. I now regret not taking it more seriously. I had little information to 'challenge' her with. What I knew about Mozart could be written on the back of a postage stamp. I have forgotten most of that regression, but one point remains firmly stuck in my memory. Shelley claimed that she had been playing with Marie Antoine, as she called her, rather than Marie Antoinette, and that Mozart had slipped on the shiny corridor floors and bumped his head. Marie Antoine picked him up and kissed him better and Mozart asked her to marry him. That was basically all that I remembered from the first of the Mozart sessions.

Shelley began to experience stronger and stronger recall of this life whilst she was conscious and became anxious to share these vivid memories with me. I questioned Shelley about her learned knowledge of classical music history, specifically pertaining to Mozart's time. But she'd been away from school with glandular fever for those lessons and never learned about them.

She came out with detailed information on Mozart. I began to feel I was doing her a disservice listening to her talk about his life and not being able to validate any of it. I finally went to the library and got a number of books out about him, but my clinic work started to pile up on me around that time and I had to put them aside, regrettably, for some time.

One day she wanted to watch the video of 'Amadeus' which had recently been released and wanted to know what I thought. I replied that she was welcome to see it but please remember that if she was hoping to be taken seriously as Mozart, people would say she'd cribbed her knowledge from the movie.

She huffed off, saying she didn't care about who believed what. Feeling the need to make it up to her I sprinted down to Bob's Video Shop in Ardleigh Green Road and snapped up a copy. Shelley and my kids settled in the front room and excitedly loaded the video to see what all the fuss was about.

After a short while I had to take an urgent phone call. The call itself was interrupted by Shelley's shrill voice calling me.

Shelley, though left-handed, wrote this signature as Mozart with her right hand.

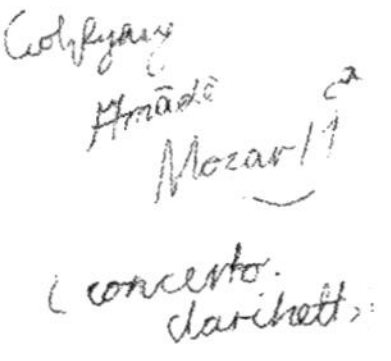

Mozart's original signature

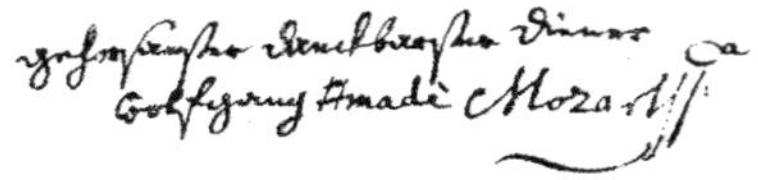

Excusing myself to the caller, I ran into the front room where Shelley was sitting with the remote control pointing at the freeze framed movie and she exclaimed with an air of superiority, 'Look! I told you so!'

Bringing the film once more to life with a purposeful click, we witnessed the scene where Mozart visits the Emperor, some time in his mid twenties.

'But he's not six, is he –'

'Shush, Dad,' my son said. 'Listen.'

The Emperor in the film spoke: 'Mozart, do you remember when you visited the palace with your sister Nannerl when you were six, and you fell off the piano and my daughter picked you up and kissed you better and then you asked her to marry you? Do you remember?'

Shelley turned to me.

'Well,' I hesitated. 'It is amazing what we've just seen and heard, but you actually said the corridor and the Emperor said you fell from the piano.'

'The movie's wrong. I slipped on the floor in the corridor. Do you believe everything you see in movies?'

I left the room suitably chastised.

Over the next few days, spurred on as much by the wrong things in the film as the right ones, Shelley began to have more and more conscious recollection of Mozart's life. And I began to find time to study the books about the great man.

In one of the books, I found the first piece of startling evidence, that he had indeed slipped on the corridor's surface just as Shelley had claimed all along. The film was wrong!

Following this great news I apologised to Shelley and threw myself into the study of Mozart's incredible life with great zeal. Speaking to her amazed parents we found more corroborative evidence that there indeed may be good reason to believe that Shelley was not mistaken. At age five Shelley and her brother Sam were taken to the local piano teacher, Mrs Challis. The very first time that Shelley sat at the keyboard Mrs Challis proudly proclaimed to their parents that this is potentially the finest pianist I have ever seen. Sam is very good too. As good as they were, they both seemed to make heavy going of the whole thing and despite the weekly lessons and regular home practice they never moved beyond Grade 2 in 5 years. After deliberating on this point and learning how much poor Mozart had suffered for his art I sensed that this was the reason for the lack of advancement. Shelley had the skill but was reluctant to use it. Much hardship and misery ensued from Mozart's talents, only to land him in an early grave.

It was no secret that although she loved her younger brother, she was not as close to Sam as she could be. Through the next regression (how could we resist), we were to get a fascinating insight into where this enmity may have had its origin.

At the end of the session, true to her forthright nature, Shelley blurted out, 'No wonder I never liked him. Sam was Nannerl. She gave me such a hard time as Mozart. She was consumed with envy over my superior skills on the keyboard. She drove me nuts as a kid...'

Those issues that are unresolved, as you may already know, follow us from life to life as often do the souls that we have these issues with. Friends come back as well-wishers, old enemies return as our adversaries or we as theirs.

By this time I had read just about everything I could lay my hands on regarding Mozart's life. When I discovered something that she had claimed happened and I could find no reference to it, I sought more books until I found the confirmation, but nothing could prepare me for the shock contained in the concluding pages of the last book I read.

There, within the book's pages was the actual same signature that left-handed Shelley had furnished me with on her first session in April 1986. The misspelt name, or so I had concluded, and done with her right hand too. There it was in all its silent mis-spelt glory.

Why the wrong spelling of his own name?

Mozart, I was to learn, was greatly given to fun, mischief and distraction and often changed his names, writing Amade, Amadeo or Amadeus and indeed Mozart sometimes with one two or three ts.

During this period I was lecturing at Cambridge University on reincarnation. I had shown the two compelling signatures to an audience of over 200 students at Trinity one evening before a regression experiment. The next time I visited Cambridge, Shelley was very keen to come with me, just to see what I got up to there. The programme was to be held in Wolfson College. When the participants saw that Shelley was accompanying me, some of the students who were there at Trinity that night asked if she were Mozart. Somewhat embarrassed that I had led her into a situation that exposed her to unwanted and prying attention, I answered politely in the affirmative, hoping nothing more would be said. Brushing it quickly aside, I began with the evening's lecture which explained the subtle nuts and bolts of the transmigratory process, followed by case histories and finally, mass hypnosis.

Just prior to the final segment, a hand went up and a young

man called out, 'Why don't we skip the mass regression and regress Mozart instead?'

I tried to fob him off and darted a few apologetic glances in Shelley's direction.

More students started to call out, until almost everyone became involved. I looked again at Shelley who remained stoically unfazed by it all. She seemed to be enjoying the attention. Then she raised her eyebrows in mock resignation and graciously consented. A spirited cheer went up as the plucky youngster stood up and bravely headed for the central seat that I had just vacated and calmly sat down without a trace of apprehension.

Someone in the audience had nipped out and come running back into the hall, clutching what looked like a book which contained the complete collection of Mozart's letters. Approaching me with a mischievous grin on his crafty young face he opened the book randomly to a letter.

'Thank you,' I said, through clenched teeth, outwardly feigning gratitude and inwardly mouthing: you bloody smart arsed toff.

Can you conceive of a test more stringent than this?

He points to the date and time on the letter and says, 'Take her there, if you can, that is.' Smiling wryly, he slunk back to his seat.

And so we began. At first I took her back to no particular time in Mozart's life to familiarize her with the vibration and ambience of that personality and then, I took her to the time written on the letter. I saw that it was written to his cousin Marie Anne Thekla, a name that I had never heard Shelley utter. I told her the time and date, and asked, 'What are you doing at this moment?'

'I'm writing a letter to my cousin Marie Anne Thekla.'

I couldn't resist a quick, smarmy glance in my little toff's direction.

'What's he say in the letter?' he quietly mouthed.

'Mozart, what's in the letter?

Shelley/Mozart started shaking with unstoppable mirth and this continued growing in intensity, for around 30 seconds, when suddenly it erupted into the most infectious belly holding howl, so strong that she began to tip off the chair. I rushed forward and caught her before she slipped completely off. Steadying her, I asked, 'Mozart? What's in the letter?'

A moment passed and then she replied hesitantly as though she was a little embarrassed, 'I'm telling my cousin how many different ways you can go to the toilet.'

This time the audience erupted into laughter and Mozart remained silent as if not hearing them. I looked at the toff to gauge his response at her astonishing statement. He nodded in sober agreement with what Shelley had said, and then shook his head incredulously.

Reading quickly down, flushed with this astonishing success, I confidently posed the next question. 'Anything else, Wolfgang? Is there something else you might share with us?'

'We're in the beer cellar and we've finished our wine and we're filling the empty bottles with our piss and leaving them for the drunks!'

More laughter from Mozart and audience alike. Shelley was one hundred percent correct. She had furnished us all with the details that were written in the book of Mozart's letters. Everyone, including myself, was stunned.

Pleased as a veritable punch I brought Shelley back to full waking consciousness. The toff was now visibly shaken by the phenomenal accuracy. Was it really Mozart's reincarnation sitting in the chair amongst all of us mind-blown adults as nonchalant as she had been during the hypnosis? Was it really the great man himself? The person who the Guinness Book of World Records says is the most played and recorded composer in the world?

Now more composed, this converted inquisitor theatrically closed the book that had been the source of our difficult questions and joyfully pronounced, 'Shelley either has a PhD in Mozart's life or she damn well is him!'

Everybody clapped and Shelley took an exaggerated bow and on the wave of euphoria we distributed a good number of copies of the *Bhagavad Gita* wherein all this cosmic information concerning the process of reincarnation and so much more was contained and explained at length.

The more I got to investigate this truly stupendous case the more the proof seemed to be amassing on the side of the affirmative.

Sometimes she would say things that I would have to research, but always the correct answers were given.

Then Shelley took the whole shebang up another notch when she involved me personally in that dazzling, beleaguered life.

'You were my friend back then. I know you. I loved you. You had a beautiful broad smile, just like a banana.'

'Oh,' I said, never even slightly daring to doubt her now. 'So who was I?'

'Thomas Linley,' she replied as if I should already know.

'Who's he?' I had to ask.

'He was my English friend, we met I think when we were both on tour in Europe. You were a child. So was I. You played wonderful violin.'

Then suddenly Shelley paused, a tear began to form in the corner of her eye and she began to quietly weep. 'You drowned. You drowned in England. You fell in...'

'We're here in happier times now. Let it go. Breathe it away. After all, God has brought us back together again...'

Later I began my search through relevant books to see if I could find corroborating evidence and sure enough, before very long, there it was. Thomas Linley, infant prodigy violinist, drowned in a boating accident in Grimethorpe Castle lake at the age of 23. Due to his virtuoso musical skills and his outstanding compositions he was affectionately named the English Mozart.

He was a childhood friend of the great composer and had met and played with Mozart whilst on tour in Europe.

Fourteen

I CAME TO UNDERSTAND the regression process was beneficial not only to give folk faith that there is no such thing as death but also to release previous trauma from their subtle body, thus healing and enlivening the present existence, as I witnessed with Irene.

Another fascinating aspect that one is likely to experience during regression is the heightened state of consciousness that attends it, whereby the regressee can know who other folk are and were, for example, Shelley recognising me as Thomas Linley. This is a common phenomenon.

I learned that the ancient Indian manuscripts name the source of information that flows through each living entity as Paramatma or Supersoul. Supersoul is said to be an expansion of God, present not only in the heart but in every one of the atoms that are scattered throughout the universe. Therefore, the Supersoul is said to be fully aware of the whereabouts and activities of everyone

There are many rules to help us pass through this life as safely as possible. Driving a car, for instance, can be a life-enhancing experience, yet there are many rules to help keep ourselves safe. There are thousands of instructions to aid and abet our transportation process. Similarly, the spiritual literatures of the world, it seems to me, are also there to assist our journey through life. Just as there are different classes of people at different stages of spiritual evolution, there are also different religious processes to benefit that group of souls' needs at that time.

With regards to death, I was interested to know that if we make our appearance on this side aided by midwives and loving relatives, are we also aided on the return journey?

June, a friend of Helen and Bobby, was suffering from bone cancer. Shortly before she fell ill she became a committed Christian and received baptism. I offered to go to her house each week and give her relaxation techniques to help cope with the increasing pain. I brought with me my latest CD of soft healing Krishna chants which June used to like very much even though it wasn't necessarily from a Christian source. She was a simple and open-minded soul.

Several months down the line, the dreaded news came that the disease was terminal. June wasn't told. Toward the end, she was taken in to the Oncology ward at Romford's Oldchurch hospital, where I would visit weekly on days when her family couldn't make it in.

One particular day, June said out of the blue, 'Hey, John, do you think I could die from this?'

I didn't feel it was up to me to say, so I said ambiguously, 'June, all of us have to go sooner or later.' Things were looking bleak and, to make things worse, the ward was drab and miserable, everyone weighed down by the inevitable. And worse still, each time I began to do some sort of relaxation or gentle massage of June's feet, an old lady a few beds up would shout at me for not helping her. Instead of responding positively to the insults I chose perhaps wrongly to ignore her and get on with helping June

One week, I found June sitting up, bright-eyed and excited to talk, despite the fact that some of her bones had begun to break, her arm was in a sling and her pain was increasing. I commented on her bright smile and her shiny eyes and she replied very excitedly, that she had experienced a most wonderful dream. Firstly she was approached by the western version of what Vedic literature refers to as Yamadutas. And what I refer to as the messengers of the Lord of Death. They were disguised as members of, would you believe it, the A Team, some gun-toting, muscle-bound, good guys from an old TV series. They asked her if she'd like to come with them and she indignantly replied, 'No, thank you very much.'

At that moment the lady in the bed directly beside her popped into the dream and said she'd love to come and they duly took her instead. As the dream continued, she heard a voice within her heart, and it said that he was very pleased with the way she was dealing with the situation she found herself in. He asked if she was satisfied to continue on with her Christian path, or whether she'd like to experience God as I do. She thought about it for a while and said she would like to try what John does. At that moment she was surrounded by some Hare Krishna devotees and she danced and chanted with them in ecstasy for the remainder of the night.

'Look,' June cried out. 'Take a look around the ward. It's shining, can't you see?' Well, yes, it was shiny but I put that down to it being a sunny day. 'They're all smiling, John. Did you ever see that before?' It had to be said everyone did seem to be smiling. 'Look here she comes!'

The old lady who had always screamed abuse at me reached the end of June's bed and I braced myself for the usual tirade. Astonishingly she beamed a smile as warm as the sun.

'You looking after Junie, darling? God bless ya, God bless ya.'

And she walked off.

'See John? I'm telling you, that dream has changed everything,' said June, happily.

It really had. June was peaceful, fearless and invigorated.

Two weeks later, Brian, June's husband, called to say she

was gone. As he tearfully expressed the great loss of his dear wife there seemed to be something in his voice that was expressing hope. I asked Brian about the actual passing. He replied that he never thought he could ever feel a sense of upliftment at a passing but he had. I was very happy for them that they were all there with her at the time, and I asked, 'So did the hospital call you to tell you she was slipping away?'

'No. Each one of us independently felt a strong urge to see June and we made our separate ways there.' When they had all arrived, June seemed quite fine and they made their loving exchanges. Then, fixing her deep brown eyes toward the end of the bed, June suddenly said, 'Oh, here's Jesus.' She reached out, and her life on Earth was over.

Around two weeks later as I was awakening and in that space halfway between asleep and awake, I heard an emphatic voice:

'John? John? It's June. It's me.'

'June?'

'Yes, John, I want to tell you something wonderful. Jesus has been taking care of me nicely and he's arranging for me to be born in a Krishna devotee family. Isn't it wonderful? Thank you, John. I've got to go.'

When I met Brian some time later we again went into depth about the amazing story of June and during that feeling of intimacy I told him what had happened in my 'dream'. I didn't really know what to expect from him and I think he didn't know how to react to it either. He might have been a little surprised or upset that he wouldn't be seeing her again. But in my experience souls who have an unfulfilled mandate of love are brought back again, sometimes in the same families, sometimes as friends, sometimes even as children or grandchildren to the beloved they have recently left.

In my experience it seems to depend upon the Karmic bank balance that each soul has created. It may be that they will meet again but in the next or in a number of lives, and if the 'material' that they have between them; enmity, debts, lust, frustration has been exhausted, mutually cleared or forgiven, their paths may never again meaningfully cross.

Everything is based on desire. A cruel dictator may be want to continue as leader of many, so in his next life his desires to lord it over many souls may be fulfilled by making him king of an ant hill in the country that he once ruined.

In the Vedic literature Jesus is known as Iswara Putra (Son of God). He is one of the many *Avatars*, divine beings who take birth on Earth, each one of them exhibiting unique and unexcelled power and morality which positively enhances the consciousness of the human race.

The wonderful idea that Lord Jesus, as in June's case, would personally participate in bringing each soul closer to their chosen understanding of God is remarkable. The divisive thinking that we are taught and brought up with - that we alone are right whether it be in secular or spiritual life – has nothing to recommend it. That of course applies to me too.

How we live our lives seems to determine what kind of consciousness we have at the time of departure. That then becomes the blueprint of our next life. Whether the blueprint denotes liberation or incarceration is completely up to us.

I have spoken to nurses who work in hospital wards where the terminally ill are cared for. They have shared many stories with me that have confirmed that often the departing soul has acted in a way that would indicate that there were unseen beings who seemed to be in attendance at the final moments, creating an atmosphere of confidence and joy, or sometimes the very opposite where they have experienced the departing soul become suddenly terrified at what they alone could see.

Each major religious tradition has slightly different takes on it, but the nurses seemed to indicate that these pre-death dispositions were common to all races and creeds. Furthermore, all the world's great religions seem to share somewhat similar processes whereby piety or impiety is measured and rewarded appropriately following death.

What I've observed from my work with thousands of regression experiences over a twenty-five year period is that those who have not attained self realization and who have within their hearts the desire to continue to enjoy in this world, which I guess is quite a few of us, are met at time of death by the Yamadutas.

Yama is the name of the demigod in charge of death and Duta means servant. What leaves the dead physical body is the subtle counterpart made of finer elements than the fleshy tabernacle. These elements are known as mind, intelligence and ego. The soul is still trapped within the subtle body and will remain so, life after life, until liberation.

I wondered what kind of departure Mozart encountered, taking into consideration his bizarre antics.

According to my young American friend, Mozart suffered at the hands of the Yamadutas. This must have been due to his mischievous nature. Shelley described how 'these really ugly half-men, half-monsters dragged me out and right on the spot, broke all my fingers and then tore every hair out of my head in bloody painful clumps.'

As shocked as I was to learn of Mozart's brutal disembarkment, I couldn't help wondering why they seemed to specifically target those bodily parts. I took to reading again and found a passage that focused on Mozart's appearance. Although Mozart himself was of plain appearance, he did possess beautifully elegant hands and wonderful brown hair to which he was very attached. So we can just imagine how much pride he had stored up in such possessions making them a natural target for the Yamadutas.

So, how does a Mozart become a Mozart? Again the clues

came from the Gita and writings of the sadhus (saintly persons) and of course Shelley's first hand experiences. Two births prior to the soul of Shelley being covered with Mozart's consciousness, she lived in India and was a sun-god worshipper named Narayan. She worshiped the sun-god Surya as her Ishta Deva or beloved chosen deity. Hinduism is a vast culture, and belief systems within that culture range from ancestor worship, ghost worship, demigod worship, to Brahman, the imperishable non-dual white light, as well as worship of Rama and Krishna, probably the two most popular deities on the Indian sub-continent.

As Narayan she worshiped the demigod of the sun. It is understood in Hindu culture that those who worship the demigods will have their next life in the demigod realms, while those who worship ghosts and spirits will go to them. It is also understood that those who worship God will not enter into the previously mentioned interim states but will come home to Godhead forever.

Shelley was partaking of a lesser form of worship which as we will see definitely bore the fruit she longed for, but sadly there were some other fruits to taste which were not so palatable.

She was a devotee of Surya (the demigod presiding over the sun) and the way she spoke in such loving devotional terms was very touching. I asked her to go to the most wonderful time in that life and she quickly responded by saying that she was sitting in the top of a tree, overlooking the Ganges, watching her beloved red-gold lord as he gracefully dipped below nightfall's enchanting horizon and then she broke into spontaneous prayer which sounded to me like Sanskrit. I wrote it down there and then, but due to the passage of time and the thought that I would never write a book in my life I mislaid them. When I asked Narayan to translate for me into English, my wife (whom I called in to witness this amazing spectacle) and I were stunned at the sheer beauty of the prose.

True to the statements in the *Gita*, at time of death Narayana was transferred to the demigod abode of the sun. Oh, now I'm in trouble, just when you were starting to believe me. The sun? Yes, the sun. No, Rupert Murdoch wasn't there. The other sun.

How can someone live on the sun? Simply, they have a subtle body which is grouped about the mind. Not a physical one as we have here. Does the mind, (the subtle body) experience pain and burning when we think of the intense heat? No. Not at all. The sun is reputedly, one of the many heavenly planets within the material world. There are also the spiritual planets which are said to lie in a domain outside this universe.

For many years Shelley became the third wife of an aristocratic personality on the sun and lived the opulent palace life with all its concomitant luxury and privilege.

For many years she enjoyed the good karma that she had accrued as Narayan until it was finally spent. She then had to return to our world and enter the womb of Frau Mozart, still hearing the wonderful music of those heavenly climes playing in her ears.

Mozart never had to cross out any of his compositional notation, he just wrote it as he heard it. I would go so far as to say he never really composed anything. He just recorded the God-given music that he had been privileged to hear.

I would hasten to venture that nothing is ours. Everything is on loan for a period of time. Those who have amassed, due to superior behaviour in a previous existence, pious credits that allow them to be empowered with extraordinary talent, beauty or wealth, are then expected to responsibly utilize it. Others, it seems, due to their impious credits, are likewise expected to deal with the incumbent Karmic millstone until time mercilessly enforces it and then mercifully releases it from their humbled necks.

Fifteen

SEVERAL ANCIENT CULTURES have preserved knowledge concerning the many dimensions within our world of which people today are completely unaware or completely dismissive. We are fairly ignorant even about those things we can see, touch and hear, let alone those we can't. There are many things that exist that we can't see: music, microbes, TV and radio waves, electricity, and so on and so forth.

And so it is for spirits or ghosts. Whether we can see them or not, whether we believe or not, whether we want them or not, the unseen ghostly realms co-exist alongside our tangible world of so-called 'reality'. This is the realm where the dead live. We could call it the Land of Never Say Die.

My experiences have led me to the conclusion that a ghost is merely a person who no longer possesses a physical form. They feel, think and act in very much the same way as they did when they inhabited a physical form, but they exist now in a subtle body.

As they had needs on the earth, they also have needs and desires in these realms too. Often they much prefer the physical realms over their own, and so we are 'visited' time and time again by these characters, so that their 'thirsts' can be slaked, their habits fed and their desires fulfilled. In the most part they are frustrated in this endeavour. They climb in bed with their widow but sadly she does not see them. They sit in their old beloved chair by the fire, but the dog jumps on top of them. They fit themselves into a picture or painting so as to have a body of sorts, and watch helplessly as time passes and their loved ones move on. Some of them, who have a little subtle power, knock over a vase to attract attention. Some manifest the smell of the cigarettes or tobacco they smoked, perfume worn. These are known as hauntings.

These souls are the ones that have not yet passed on to the process of reincarnation, though one day the opportunity will come. These are the folk who have strong attachments to their habits, to their relatives and homes, and are bound in that half-world to wander aimlessly.

Some are luckier in their attempts to penetrate our realm. We allow or even inadvertently encourage them in this by breaking our protective aura. This happens through drugs, alcohol and the abuse of sexuality.

These base activities summarily weaken the etheric surroundings and the 'cracks' that appear in it allow them to enter into our consciousness. They use our bodies to continue what death terminated. Ultimately, we are not only fighting our own gross desires but also their subtle ones.

This is what I have learned in my many years of working with the haunted and addicted. You have every reason to be cynical, but I have no reason to lie or try to mislead you.

Cold Turkey is that point where the body is struggling to regain its pre-substance abuse status as the unhealthy environment established by it wages war on its former owner. So on the physical level, a chemical war is taking place, but on an unseen level, there is an even more intense metaphysical battle raging between the minds of the ghost and the host. The ethereal guests are cursing, screaming, cajoling, threatening, and above all doing their damnest, and believe me it is their damnest, to confuse, to halt the imminent ejection, as they are repelled from their hosts auric surround.

Unless the host quickly goes about repairing, by good clean living, the cracks that their former activities created, the ghosts will most certainly return. They are a nasty bunch and you mess with them at your peril. Hard and soft drug takers, big boozers, whatever gets you through the night dudes – beware.

Have you ever seen a very nice pleasant person enter a pub at 8 o'clock and by 11 pm, after sinking a gut full he wants to kill anyone or everyone? The next day he is back to his pleasing self and shocked to hear of how he wanted to murder one of his best friends the boozy night before.

Ghosts again. They are literally hanging from the rafters waiting to fall into the disintegrating auras of the merry-makers below. They know it is only a matter of time before they will be spending a very happy night with their victim, under their control and doing their nefarious bidding.

From 1984 till 2004 we hosted a Sunday Love programme, as it is called in Krishna speak, at our home in Hornchurch, Essex. Being an open-house policy, we attracted some great and some not so very great souls into our living room.

My daughter, Pia, who was highly psychic, said, 'Dad, see that new chap?'

'Which one?'

'Billy. He's got about seven ghosts on him.'

'Really? Is he taking anything?'

'Hash.'

'Ok. I'll have a gentle word.'

When the opportunity presented itself, I made small talk, and eventually asked if he smoked. He said no, and seemed to be sincerely committed to a clean, healthy way of life.

'That's one of the reasons for coming around to the programme,' he told me.

My daughter was having none of it.

'Ask him about Sunday mornings in the potting shed,' she

insisted. 'That's where he's growing it and smoking it.'

Trying not to be too confrontational, I approached him with a twinkle in my eye.

'Bill, perhaps you don't know but some of the Hare Krishnas are advanced enough to distinguish reality from illusion.'

'What do you mean?' he asked, looking a little alarmed.

'The potting shed, Bill. On Sundays isn't it?'

'How did you know?'

'My daughter can see how fractured your aura is. She also sees around seven vampires feeding off you.'

'Vampires?'

'They may as well be. Ghosts like to share the habit with you. Seven of them. They're all wanting a little piece of you.'

Bill went from the crimson-red of lie telling, to the ashen white of pre-flight fright. Knowing now that he was being watched when he came to our house in the afternoon, and had 'used' prior to that in his green-house, Bill burned his plants and in a short period, via chanting mantras and eating healthy vegetarian food, his aura healed and the spirits went in search of another victim.

Sometimes the ghosts don't go elsewhere, but stay right there in the victim's house as uninvited guests.

A prominent public speaker stopped by with his daughter one day and asked if I could do anything for her. She was addicted to heroin and he was naturally beside himself with anxiety for her.

These sorts of therapies are very difficult as the inevitable ghosts on board are very committed to keeping things just how they want them. Often when someone finally decides enough is enough and they want to try to stop, these voices vehemently rise up and convince the victim otherwise. I know you may say that is the person's own mind and to a great extent it can be so, but in every single case of curing addiction I have encountered vampiristic ghosts who threatened, cursed, and opposed it all the way.

This young lady was no exception. I am not going to go through all the nuts and bolts of the therapy as this is not a healing manual, but suffice it to say that it took something like six hours of intense confrontation to get them out, and boy were they nasty.

Maybe there are some people out there who have a more successful, easier way to eject them, but I found what eventually worked was talking to them, bartering with them, as you would with living humans; and also chanting God's names.

Shortly after, her dad arrived and gratefully they left together for their home in the West of England.

The next day was a Saturday and Pia came bowling in from London to spend the weekend resting and relaxing. After giving her Ma and Pa a warm hug she disappeared upstairs to her bedroom. She had no idea that, seeing as my clinic was not set up at this time, I'd used her room for the treatment. Seated in our downstairs lounge, just about to watch a bit of telly, I hear, boom boom boom boom, as Pia's footsteps frantically carried her down the stairs, screaming,

'Dad! Dad! What have you been doing in my room? There's a bunch of blinking druggie ghosts in there!'

I'd helped someone else's daughter and ended up disturbing my own! We purified the atmosphere with holy music and chanting the names of God.

A relative on my side of the family asked me if I could assist her son as he had been diagnosed with epilepsy. He had been experiencing grand mal 'fits' and wondered if there was anything I could do to assist.

I wasn't terribly confident that I would be of any use to her son but decided to see him on the off chance that I could.

On questioning the child about the onset of these fits he replied that they had begun around a month previous. While looking into the child's eyes I noticed what I thought to be some irregularity in the size of the pupils and thought that it was maybe the influence of the drugs he was now obliged to take. My instincts however lead me to believe there just might be some unseen factor that was responsible.

'Have you had an accident?' I asked.

'Well yes, you could call it an accident. I fell down the stairs from top to bottom.'

'Were you knocked out?'

'Kinda.'

'Was this before or after the epileptic fits started?'

'Just before.'

The pupils seemed to dilate further and I knew that it wasn't just down to drugs; he had an uninvited 'friend'.

Accidents can fracture bones and auras alike. This can provide a golden opportunity for a ghost in the vicinity to get in.

I put Leslie into a hypnotic state and invited our spectral visitor to communicate. His face began to distort into a wraith-like appearance, the chin somehow jutting forward and the mouth creasing into the visage of a nasty old crone.

No sooner had the being gained control of Leslie's body then it began acting akin to a mentally subnormal person, just groaning and moaning unintelligible words and causing him to froth at the mouth.

I began chanting mantras for his protection and then spoke firmly both to the ghost and to the immobilised youth, encouraging the child not to be afraid and that we would remove the malevolent influence very soon, while simultaneously preaching to the ghoul that there was so much better things for it to do than victimise this poor kid. I offered it an opportunity to improve its lot by looking towards heaven's light and chanting Hare Krishna.

There was no reply, just more moaning and growling so I upped the intensity, shouting the prayers with more and more strength and praying inside for God to aid us. Suddenly I realised that the ghoul was becoming as bewildered as Leslie and seemed to respond to my suggestions. I encouraged it with more excitement and force to chant the names of God and free itself.

Getting clearer and surer with every attempt and as this poor thing continued straining at the Holy Names I encouraged Leslie to 'push through' and chant behind him with the wonderful result that the intruder's moaning voice was slowly but surely replaced by Leslie's voice chanting loud and clear Hare Krishna, Hare Krishna.

Leslie sat bolt upright and asked if he had fallen asleep and why he had woken suddenly shouting Hare Krishna. Everything was explained to him to his full satisfaction. The ghost was gone.

So was the epilepsy, never to return.

Not all ghosts are malevolent, as many of you are already aware. Three very touching, special stories of child ghosts come to mind.

The first concerned a devotee called Lila who lived in Soho St Temple in the eighties.

She was complaining that each time she went in front of the altar she would feel a strong panic sweep over her and then a sensation of drowning. One day when I was visiting she begged me for assistance.

I soon discovered that she had a small, frightened visitor on board called Pepe. Pepe told me in a tiny child's voice that he lived with his father on a boat somewhere on South America's coast and that one day, when his father wasn't looking, Pepe fell overboard and drowned. For him, the whole thing, apart from being terrifying, was very confusing as his subtle body rose up out of the water and tearfully approached his distraught father thinking he would be taken lovingly and protectively into his arms. But his father couldn't see him.

After days of frustrated attempts to get his father's attention he noticed a sweet little girl walking up and down the beach. Just like him, she was lost and lonely. Although she never noticed him either, he liked her so much he stayed with her in that 'lonely' space in her aura that deeply yearned for companionship. Pepe remained there for a long time. The little girl who was hosting him was Lila who in her earlier years had lived in South America and had relocated to England when she became a Krishna devotee.

I realised that when Lila was chanting in front of the altar, Pepe was being removed by this spiritual process and, in all the confusion of losing his 'home' again, he relived his death trauma. Seeing as he was living in the girl's aura, she felt it too. I couldn't simply kick Pepe out. We had to find a home for him. But I couldn't create a new situation for Pepe. This was a case for 'Upstairs Management'.

I spoke to Pepe about God and how we could ask for help. Pepe was enthusiastic about that. Then I said, 'Pepe, would you like a nice new mummy so that you can start over again?'

'Yes, please,' he replied sweetly.

'First I'll help you go up to heaven. There'll be a gate and a nice man will speak to you there. This will be one of God's servants and I want you to say to him, 'Dear Sir, can you help me? My friend John said that you might ask God if I can have a new mummy please?'

So before he departed I told him to chant and to come and tell me what the outcome was. Lila fell silent for about five minutes as Pepe went for help.

Soon Pepe was back.

'What happened?' I asked.

'I chanted and went to heaven and there was a nice man

there and I said what you told me to say, and he went inside a big house and came back smiling and said that God is very happy to help and he said if I wanted I could look down this white tube and I would be able to see my new mummy, and so I did and guess what? She's a lovely, big, fat black lady who's going to love me a lot.'

'That's wonderful, Pepe. As you leave now, keep chanting nice and strong and everything will work out fine.'

Pepe repeated over and over again those wonderful words and second by magical second his voice became fainter and fainter as he departed for his new life. How sweet a moment it was.

Lila made an instant, full recovery and was never troubled by the drowning sensations and panic attacks again.

Around the same time, during the mid-eighties, there was a lady who came to our shop who wasn't sleeping very well. Helen, my business partner, convinced her that a session or two with me would do her the world of good.

After questioning the lady about her life, I decided to teach her some self-hypnosis so that she could deal with life's challenges at source rather than having to come to a therapist every time she got stressed and sleepless. I was never very good as a businessman.

On the third and final treatment something wonderful happened. The spirit of her Downs Syndrome child appeared to her. This very important factor had been strangely overlooked when she told me the details of her life at our first session.

At first, the lady cried at the sudden, unexpected appearance of her lost baby, but quickly the mood changed as it became obvious that there was some unfinished business between them. I thought that the business was perhaps the need to say goodbye or perhaps some unexpressed grief on the part of the mother that she needed closure on and my beloved inner guide whom I now called Supersoul were arranging such an event through me.

But no, it was not so. The mother was not looking for closure. The little baby was. The baby's words were being spoken by the mother rather than in the case of Pepe, who spoke for himself. The baby had come back to let the mother know that she was disgusted at how she had been treated. The mother then had to admit that she had been ashamed of her child's condition, so much so that she had the baby taken away at birth. She convinced her own mother to take the baby instead.

The baby passed away tragically after nine months and the mother never went to the funeral, let alone visited the grave. No wonder she couldn't sleep.

The lady then burst into tears of remorse and begged the soul of the baby for forgiveness, which she sweetly gave. In her mind, they hugged, kissed and bonded, and finally, for them both, it was over.

They had closure.

Two weeks later the lady came again to see me with the news that she was now sleeping soundly. I was glad. Then she said that, for some unknown reason, her baby's grave had never grassed over like the other children's graves on either side. The grandmother who had cared for the child throughout had regularly visited the grave over the last year and had noted, with some distress, the phenomenon. After the 'reunion' at our shop, the mother finally visited the barren grave, and there she wept more tears of remorse. On her next visit, grass had completely covered the baby's grave.

Sixteen

GERRY SLATTERY, ONE OF MY BEST FRIENDS and a great musician, became interested in spiritual life after we met in the 90s. Just prior to this, I was booked to sing on Boy George's new album along with Laura Logic, Polystyrene, Pia and one or two other devotees. After the success of *Bow Down Mister*, which brought George deservedly back into the public eye, we had appeared on many prime time TV shows and it was on one of these shows that Gerry had seen us and got the idea to use us for his recording of *Swing Low Sweet Chariot* which Gerry was going to present to West Ham football club for half-time music.

We found we had a mutual love for 50s music, especially the Everly Brothers, and after we had finished with Swing Low, we sang our favourite Everly hits for a half an hour or more, Gerry singing Don's parts and me singing Phil's.

Soon we were seeing each other regularly and recorded a number of Everly songs which I had 'Krishnised' by adjusting the lyrics. The album was entitled *The Heavenly Brothers*. It was great fun.

He encouraged me to speak openly about Krishna and it wasn't long before Gerry was an enthusiastic chanter. He also encouraged me to bring his brother Derek into Krishna Consciousness. The Slatterys were a very open minded, open hearted bunch. When I first met them, they lived on the

Thamesview Estate in Barking and had the only bakery in the small parade of shops there. They and their wives became vegetarians and learned how to meditate, Krishna style.

Derek had two daughters, one son and several cute grand children.

Of these, five year old Bonny was especially adorable. Even though her mum, Shannon, was not terribly pro-Krishna, Bonny quickly learned how to chant and dance and enjoyed the blessed food that Cherrille had prepared. Bonny used to say to me how her mummy would stop her from chanting at home when she would spontaneously break out, innocently singing Hare Krishna.

Shannon, Bonny's mum, and her sister Kath had just purchased a caravan on the coast in Essex and had gone down for the weekend to clean out and refurbish their new acquisition with Bonny in tow. While Shannon and Kath were ripping out some of the old fashioned fittings in the caravan, Bonny was playing with her plastic football outside.

Shannon had thrown the wood outside and she didn't see the piece that had a nail sticking up into the air. She was keeping one eye on Bonny all the time and saw her kick the ball up in the air and it land on the woodpile, directly onto the offending nail. Instantly the ball deflated following the sharp bang as it was punctured, preceding Bonny's wailing as her precious ball met its untimely end.

Bonny came rushing in to her mum, bawling and asking for her to do something. Her mum was naturally distracted with all the work she had to get done over the weekend and said to her that as soon as they had a minute they would go over the camp site shop and replace the ball. But no, Bonny didn't want a new ball then. She wanted her old one fixed and nothing else would do. Shannon stood her ground and wouldn't give in.

Shannon watched as Bonny went back to the wood pile.

Shannon felt a mite guilty that she had dismissed her in favour of refurbishment. Bonny didn't have a father, so mother and daughter, although very different people, were deeply entwined in one another's hearts. What follows are the actual words that anti-Hare Krishna, outspoken, strong willed, no-nonsense Shannon said to me:

'So, I'm watching Bonny through the caravan, with my sister as witness and Bonny is looking down at the punctured ball in her hands and then looking up to the sky. Again she looks down to the ball and up to the sky. Then she shouts with all her heart and mind in a pleading, soul-rending voice, 'Krishna! Krishna! Krishna!' Then I nearly shat myself. The flat ball she was holding towards the sky blew up to its original size. Bonny just smiles and says, 'Thank you,' and we rush out to check if what we'd seen was real, and I have to admit, even though it kills me to do so, it was. That ball was fully blown up, even though the hole was still visible. It had a natural feel to it, which was strange considering the un-natural way it had just re-inflated.'

Bonny was not the only child in our congregation whom had experienced a verifiable miracle.

There is a difference, however, between the miracles that are performed by Krishna and the 'miracles' that are performed by mystic yogis. To put this into perspective, I will refer to the man who brought Krishna Consciousness to the Western world, Srila Prabhupada.

He was known and revered as someone who had achieved full knowledge regarding the process of purest love of God. Not only had he received this knowledge but he also taught this knowledge all over the world when he travelled to the West in the late 60s. In a few short years he translated seventy Vedic classics on the Science of Devotion, opened over 100 temples and farm communities, and accepted thousands of disciples. Following is a short story of one of his pastimes in India in the 70s.

Prabhupada had been invited by a number of mystic yogis to take part in a convention on self-realisation in Northern India. He spoke briefly on the principles of the supreme yoga, Bhakti, or devotional service. Then, out of the blue, a challenging call came from the audience.

'Show us a miracle!'

Some 'advanced' yogis have the ability to do magical things like manifesting objects from out of thin air, or disappearing, or reading minds. Some of them encourage the vulnerable to believe that they are incarnations of Krishna or Shiva. In this way, they procure large amounts of disciples and even larger amounts of cash.

Prabhupada agreed to the demand and then requested his Western disciples who were seated within the congregation to stand.

'Here is my miracle,' he said. 'These boys and girls were only a short time ago addicted to so many unclean and ungodly habits but through the process of chanting the Lord's Holy Names and following the principles of Bhakti Yoga they have become bright and beautiful.'

Prabhupada and his disciples sat back down and the challenger was silenced. This indeed is the miracle. The other fancy magic stuff, as impressive as it may be, is doing nothing to alleviate the suffering, distress and ignorance that holds the world in its grip.

At different times I was unexpectedly blessed with knowledge of folks' previous existences. I would intuit it, or it was somehow channelled through me. Then, without telling the person my predictions, I would offer to regress them and they would furnish me with the same information as I had subtly perceived beforehand.

In the mid-nineties I attended a mass regression seminar at the Mind Body Spirit show at the Floral Halls, Westminster. I wanted to see how others were working in this field and perhaps pick up some extra skills or techniques. Unfortunately I found the presentation a little underwhelming.

Much had been spoken about how wonderful this particular American gentlemen's gifts were. However, most of the seminar was getting us to literally guess the previous existences of the people we were sitting next to, so it was open house for any one to say any damn thing they wanted. I felt this was a tad speculative if not a mite risky, considering that what we are told when our hearts are open and trusting can have a deep and lasting impression.

There were about five hundred people there who were all ordered to turn their chairs into circles of eight and then choose who you had the clearest idea about. It was a bit of a shambles and not the most constructive and fulfilling way to entertain a crowd of people paying twenty quid each. However, people love to talk as much as they like to be talked about, so away we went.

Most didn't have very much to say and those who did didn't seem to be very confident of the content of their revelations. Then it came to the turn of (a slightly disgruntled) yours truly.

'We are not sitting together by chance, you know,' our leader soberly proclaimed, which, of course, is true.

I started with the lady next to me and asked her, 'How will you know if something I give you is true or false?'

She replied that she would see how it felt.

The spoilsport in me replied, 'Fair enough, but in my experience sometimes we feel something very strongly but later find out we were mistaken.'

So I tried to explain that once you have a 'feeling' for who someone was, you should put it to one side and then simply attempt to give information about the present life of the person you are reading first. A good amount of the personality, habits, attitudes, repulsions and attractions from the previous life are present in this one. If we are correct in furnishing each other with a picture of this life's attributes then we may posit with confidence the past personality from whom it came. Or conversely do it the other way round. Working on the present life's attributes and nature and extrapolate that on to a likely image of the past. That should only be done though if the person we are reading for gives positive feedback on the information we have provided.

I chose the lady sitting next to me first and told her what I thought might be the things she liked to do; the kind of company she preferred; the types of food and drink that she favoured; the countries she would like to live in – in short everything that fitted around the image I had in my mind of her previous existence as an aristocratic lady living in France at the turn of the 18th century.

She was quite impressed, but a young girl in her mid twenties was not.

'Lets see what you pick up for me then?' she challenged.

My false ego rose to my throat and I agreed without thinking.

I went into silence for a few seconds and a picture came of a young political activist and freedom fighter from the South Americas. This person was also a prominent pugilist, although I could not, for the life of me, say who it was. I told her that I had an idea who she was and that I would not say so until she had said yes to every one of my points regarding her present life. If she disagreed she must say so. She silently nodded.

'In this life you hate injustice. It could even bring you to the point of physical use of force unless you are very careful. You have always been a person to lock horns with authority even when you knew you were wrong. Your father was like that but it actually doesn't come from him. Your temper is yours. You were 'given' him by karma as he fulfils some need you have to surround yourself with that type of energy so as to justify the churned way you feel inside. Stop me as soon as I am wrong.'

She said nothing.

'In this life you feel as though you have been born in the wrong country and I want to suggest the South Americas, specifically Argentina and Mexico. Freedom politically for all and even more so, for the individual. A hatred of the church, but love of spirituality is burning away inside you but how to harness the physical frustrations of a 'charged' body with the strong yearnings for spiritual emancipation? These things have caused you much frustration in this life and while there's a yearning to be acknowledged as a champion of the people and accepted by all, you are nonetheless a consummate loner. You tried to heal it by diving into sex with all kinds of partners, but that just confused things more.'

At this her tears flowed silently.

'So you took up boxing, which is a rather unusual thing for me to claim, seeing as you're not particularly sporty looking neither is your nose or face any indicator.'

She smiled at that.

'You were a freedom fighter in the Americas. You were also a top notch boxer and frustrated that you were born into this female body where you can't express yourself quite as potently as you did previously. So how's that sound?'

She was astonished. All the points I'd made, including the unlikely fact that she was a member of a ladies' boxing club, were indeed true. I have to say, even was I a tad taken back. It is not that I go around sussing everybody out effortlessly. When the Upstairs deems it appropriate, it happens.

I was going back and forth to Cambridge University between 1985 to 1988 visiting the students and doing my regression thing. One week I was going to demonstrate at the venerable Christ's College.

Cambridge is set in the midst of Fenland countryside, still mystic and timeless. It is a city of contradictions – ancient buildings, antique carvings, dark narrow passageways, as well as open spaces. College gardens provide the eye with beauty and the soul with peace. Churches offer sanctuary from the daily bustle. The river Cam, fringed with hoar frost or drowsy with summer's warmth, offers quite riverside walks.

When I first walked the cobble stoned streets that precede the entrance to Christ's College I was unaware of just how great an honour it was for an uneducated person to stand before its young intelligentsia and give forth the wisdom that I had not earned as they had, but had been thrust unsuspecting upon me. I was nervous but eager to see if I could at least contribute my knowledge to its vast treasure house of learning.

We had around 150 excited students for regression at Christ College. The word had spread about the remarkable experiences that my previous work had produced. The atmosphere was buzzing, except for one young lady in her late 20s who sat right at the front in the middle, slap bang in front of me, scowling all night long. I tried my best to ignore her as there's always going to be someone who has an issue with these things, especially if the subject matter infringes uncomfortably on their belief system or faith.

I told of the experiences that I'd had over the last five years and how I believed my experiments may trace the story of the soul's birth and rebirth in the human species, as well as its development up into 'elevated life forms' or sinking down through 'lower species'. Then I showed how this principle was consistent, whatever race or creed or belief system one subscribed to.

During this, the fed-up female in the front row did her level best to put me off my stride by scowling, yawning, mumbling, smirking and the like.

Then it came to the second half of the presentation where I do a mass regression. Those who did not want to participate were welcome, I announced, to sit and watch. Around 90% of the audience took part. She didn't, of course.

During the part when we were in the past life segment she suddenly stopped scowling and for a flash of a second she closed her eyes and then opened them quickly, looking somewhat disturbed. She did this a number of times and each time, even though it literally was only a second, she began to look more and more distressed. When everyone was brought back to waking consciousness she screamed.

'Help me! Help me!' she shouted, startling all the other newly-awakened participants.

I sensed she had been unwittingly dropping in and out of trance state throughout the regression and as much as I disliked what she had been doing to me all evening, I quickly responded by taking her into a private room to preserve her dignity. I was able to put her back into the state that had preempted her distress.

Again she cried, 'Help me! Help me! I'm burning!'

She was being burned at the stake, accompanied by vengeful, hateful, chanting of 'Witch! Burn! Witch! Burn!'

I quickly took her through the death experience and cleared the trauma from her subtle body and brought her back to the relative sanctity of Christ's college.

For a few moments she wept, but within a minute, not more, she was fully recovered and finally, managed a smile, her first of the evening.

Feeling she was fully recovered I wasted no time in being gently sarcastic. 'Oh, you're smiling now, but the poor old bloke who snatched you from the fire was himself getting pilloried by you all evening. What have you got to say for yourself, young lady?'

'I'm so sorry,' she replied. 'I came tonight on a mission to see you fail. I'm a born again Christian and we believe this type of work to be that of the Devil. There is nothing about reincarnation in the Bible, let alone being taken back to previous existences and all that stuff about animals having souls, it's just too much.'

'Is it still too much?'

She paused, and then said, 'No, not any more. I truly experienced that burning and I could feel the hatred. That burned me as much as the flames.'

'So who were they?' I inquired, event though I already knew.

'Christians. Well, so-called Christians. They called me a witch because I had knowledge of herbs and suchlike and they killed me for trying to help my neighbours and friends.'

'So perhaps you've become a bit of a fanatic in this life because you're driven by the subconscious memory of this incident. You want to take shelter within that dogma because deep down if you don't you will be risking slaughter again by burning.'

She readily agreed with my hypothesis, and also agreed when I suggested that it would be likely that she might have a fear of fire in this life, as well as a dread of large noisy crowds.

I wonder how she got on with her friends at church after that, whether she 'came out' or kept the whole mind blowing experience to herself?

The very first time I demonstrated at Trinity, some three months earlier, we had around 250 folk and before I got to the end of my pitch a chap jumped up and shouted, 'This is all a load of bullshit!'

'What are you studying here?' I asked.

He proudly replied that he was a scientist.

'And what is it that scientists do? Do they experiment partially or impartially?'

'Impartially, of course,' and his facial expression silently added, 'you idiot'.

'Step out the front and let's experiment impartially.'

I was a little nervous. Usually I like to 'cherry pick' from the audience those who have the natural ability to go into trance, making it a little easier for myself. I had no idea whether this chap with his pugnacious nature would be able to do so, and then the whole evening would be in danger of going down like a lead zeppelin after the big build up our challenges had created.

Anyway, within a trice, our scientist's head lolled forward due to the cunning knock out blow of my voice which travelled unchallenged into the space between his unprotected ears and out he went.

The atmosphere was absolutely electric and I was taking him back, effortlessly, through life after fascinating life until we came to something that especially caught my attention.

'So where are you?'

'I'm living in the village of Askrigg in Yorkshire.'

'Oh, very nice. And what do you do there? Have you employment?'

'I am the vicar,' he said proudly, as proudly as he'd earlier proclaimed he was a scientist.

'Are you well read, sir?' I asked.

'Of course I am well read.' Echoes of 'you idiot' lingered still.

'So have you heard of the theory of transmigration of the soul, of reincarnation?'

He replied as if I were a piece of excrement stuck to his well-heeled boot, 'Yes of course I have.'

'Reverend, do you believe in it?'

'It is a diabolical proposition that has absolutely nothing to recommend it. No I do not!'

The audience roared with laughter. There he was, on one hand, proclaiming his adherence to one belief system and living another diametrically opposed to it.

As he regained his present day consciousness I humbly asked him to also consider God when he conducted his experiments for He may be the unknown quantity that we are all seeking to identify and comprehend: the great impartial scientist who has created the unlimited variety of phenomena that we call the material cosmos.

Perceiving another soap-box moment coming on, I addressed the audience.

'He is the source of everything, therefore to know Him is to know everything. It's not just an insignificant Hare Krishna devotee speaking, but scientists like Einstein; philosophers like Descartes and Emerson, Socrates and Plato; poets and visionaries like Tennyson, Wordsworth and Shelley. Not just little old uneducated me.'

He humbly received my request and pronounced to the spectators that from this day forth he would never judge a book by its cover and always endeavour to look beyond his prejudices. The audience clapped and cheered heartily. It was a great start to another thought provoking evening.

Seventeen

TAKING AN HONEST INVENTORY of the past I could see how I'd pretty much burned my bridges as far as the old life of sex, booze and rock'n roll was concerned when I'd set out in earnest to try to build a new life built on the time honoured principles of loving service to God and to his children, known as Bhakti Yoga.

I wasn't a shaved and celibate monk living in the temple, I was a red-blooded family man who needed to earn a living, support his family and serve the peerless Upstairs Management's manifesto by endeavouring first to waken myself and then to at least try to alert other sleep-walkers from their earth-induced trance. I had a lot of waking up to do myself. I was hardly the personification of wisdom, purity or anything else come to that, but looking back I could see that I did possess one valuable commodity: enthusiasm, which is still as alive in me today as it was then.

It was this same old enthusiasm that by 1981 had helped me swiftly qualify in remedial massage and reflexology. It got our shop up and running in no time at all. Its home was on Albert Road for a couple of years and then re-located to a better position in Victoria Road. As I've said before, business was always quiet and I was giving talks and demonstrations to the local community in the hope of reaching out and attracting more clientele. And later as money became scarce I started playing five nights a week back at the old rub-a-dub-dubs.

August 1984. The first night that I was booked to speak to the Woodford Branch of the Round Table.

There were around eighty well-heeled males in the audience that night. They had been wining and dining for an hour or more, while I sat patiently by my corduroy covered massage couch, waiting for the off.

When the time came for my bit I was introduced, warmly welcomed, and invited to show my wares. I had around 30 minutes to get my pitch across which, on this particular evening, included a talk on the principles of Reflexology, which was almost unknown at the time. Then I was to do a demonstration which consisted of inviting a member of the audience suffering from one condition or other to come out and see if I could find the problem merely by touching, squeezing and rubbing their feet. This always gave the audience a hearty laugh. They were mostly good natured, but on the odd occasion, and this was one of them, you had the even odder piss-taker who just had to have a go.

I was at that point, just before calling up someone for the experiment. Unexpectedly, this chap stands up. He's a vet. He's very annoyed at the assumption that merely by touching the feet one can tell if a person has a medical problem and, worse still, actually treat that problem by rubbing on the diagnostic spot.

He then went about wrongly twisting the information I had just given by saying that if a dog is limping from a pain in his right foot it's because he's got something wrong with his right bollock. Uproarious laughter and table thumping ensued. Even I, on the receiving end, could see the funny side of it. But when the boys had had their fun and the laughter had eventually subsided, I answered, being in the same mode of passion as he, that vets are fixated on bollocks because they earn so much money removing them, but no-one could ever castrate him because he kept his safely in the space between his ears.

That went down even better than his jibe and touché, we were even. Thankfully he shut up and let me get on with the hard bit, which was finding out what hidden problem the volunteer on the couch had. We are well aware that humans have a sense of humour, but just observe how hilarious God is, and how he has hand picked the patient so perfectly for me. The person who stepped forward was a good looking, trim, prematurely-grey man around 35 years of age. You could not detect any physical impairment as he stepped forward, totally unperturbed, took off his smart brogues and lay down on my pillowed couch.

Silence fell. The nature of these types of presentations is such that you have to come up with something quickly or you lose the audience.

Before I declared to the audience what our kind subject was suffering from, I asked his permission to make public what I'd found. He graciously agreed and so I turned and spoke, not knowing if the young silver haired man was going to agree with any of my findings.

The audience waited expectantly.

'I have to say that I'm unable to say what, exactly, this young man's problems are, but I can say with confidence, where they are. You have a problem in the left temporal lobe, which feels like it may have been there for quite some time.'

The young man's face creased with a kindly smile and sitting up on his elbows said those magic words, 'Yes. I have left temporal lobe epilepsy.'

A shock wave palpably passed through the audience.

'Now, this is a little more personal,' I continued.

You could cut the atmosphere with a knife.

'This is a subject that's already received more than its share of exposure this evening. You have a problem with your left testicle, too.'

Pandemonium broke out. Bedlam, uproar, call it what you like but God's joke tickled them twice as much as our mortal offerings. When calm restored itself, they became hushed, waiting eagerly for my volunteer's response.

'I have left testicular atrophy. It has never developed properly.'

The audience was suitably impressed. It was a wonderful experience and one of course worth giving a plug in the book. But it was not to end there. A half hour later, as I was preparing to go, this same young man, Dave, approached me with some questions about vegetarian diet and the pros and cons of it. While discussing these matters he pointed out that two or three years earlier he had been at the peak of his physical and mental powers, and was Maggie Thatcher's bodyguard for a good period of time till he succumbed to the temporal lobe epilepsy.

'Wow,' I said. 'Maggie Thatcher? What was she like?'

'Oh, she was quite nice if you got to know her. You know they called her the Iron Lady, but actually she was very sponge like.'

'Sponge like. What does that mean?' I asked.

'Well, to give you some small idea of what I mean, just imagine: I'm strong, fit as a fiddle; in the prime of my life. I almost felt invincible. Taking care of such an important personality was a great source of personal pride to me. I loved it all. All except one aspect of the job; when she touched me. We would be walking through a crowd, me slightly in front, feeling quietly proud, vigilant, sharp and then...'

He paused.

'Sometimes even the Iron Lady would get nervous, especially when crowds pushed in. She would grab hold of my hand for support.'

'How's that a problem?'

'Every bit of energy emptied out of me. She sponged it, so to speak. It happened on several occasions and every time it did, all my energy disappeared. All of it, and I was a fit lad. It just vanished. Then I started to have the fits and had to retire.'

This kind of account goes to show that interactions between people exist not only on the physical level but also on the subtle. Newspaper cartoons showed pictures of Margaret Thatcher with her cabinet members depicted as lap dogs submissively licking up to her in the corridors of power. She had a potency that no-one could, at least for a period of time, eclipse. Yet from the outside she looked just like any other person. Powerful subtle energies manifest themselves in ways we cannot always comprehend.

When I had our therapy sessions in the home garden clinic I always encourage the person to reflect on their life deeply and honestly so we can uncover the sources of their problems and how best to deal with them. One interesting session, highlighting the power of the mind to make or break someone's life, took place with a woman named Sarah.

Sarah, full of embarrassment and shame, admitted to me that she hated her daughter. From the moment she got up in the morning until the moment she left the house it was all-out war. Then the moment she slammed the front door again after school it continued until merciful bedtime. Sarah even admitted that it got so bad sometimes she wished she would never wake up.

I asked Sarah to temporarily forget the unhappiness she experienced with her daughter and reflect back on her own past. This, by the way, is not a blow by blow account of how the therapy was conducted, but a summary, calling the most important aspects of it to attention. Sarah's childhood was a miserable one with a strict, emotionally distant father and a mother somewhat out of touch with her feelings. She was an only child and they were quite poor, making do with just the bare essentials like most post-war families. She was shy, lonely and somewhat withdrawn. When she came to her early teens she cherished a great desire to live, reach out, love and be loved – to have girlfriends and a boyfriend or at least to harbour the fantasy of one. However, that was not going to happen for she was half paralyzed with fear and riddled with insecurity. She began to hate herself, viewing everything about her very existence as obnoxious.

As the painful teen years rolled on however, Sarah found herself turning slowly but surely from the ugly duckling she thought she was, into a very fine swan indeed and she married the boy she loved, who provided her with two healthy children, a nice big house in a salubrious neighbourhood and money to spend on a therapist to find out why she hated her daughter.

After we evaluated her life together, she learned to accept that it was not really her daughter she hated, but herself. When I asked her the time that these strong feelings against her daughter had arisen, she answered tearfully that they had especially magnified around her early teens. This had been the most excruciating period of Sarah's own life. To rub salt in the wound, Sarah's annoying daughter had the opportunities and facilities that Sarah could not even dream about as a kid; nice house, nice Dad, nice clothes...

I set about healing those early days and helping Sarah accept that poor little waif and stray within her by communicating with her inner child. Once she had embraced the warts-and-all teenager she once was, and once the last tears that she was ever going to shed on that period of her life were dry, we set about healing the rift with her daughter.

I asked whether her daughter would be at home or at school at that moment.

'School,' she replied.

'Close your eyes. Open your heart. Sense a wave or a fountain of the most glorious loving colour springing up from the depths of your loving heart.'

Sarah was a little uncertain how to do this.

'Little Sarah whom you have just embraced within your heart knows how. Or at least she knows what the longing to love feels like. So get her to create this feeling within your heart. Imagine you are her at the time when her heart is longing for a friend or a lover.'

Sarah's eyes moisten a little.

'Now get her to help you to visualise all the beautiful things that you as an adult have forgotten. The colours of a rainbow. The magical opening of a fragrant flower. The soaring up into the sky of this fragrant rainbow of love from your heart's centre, reaching out, reaching out, searching for a little girl who is very special, who is in need, great need of her mother's unconditional love. Look, there she is below, at her school desk, working hard at her life. She has as many dreams and hopes as you had. Feel it. See it pouring down, immersing her, supporting her, cleansing her heart of the tired poverty-stricken, love-barren energies that you had inadvertently placed around her. Wash them, cleanse them away. Replace all that was with all that is and will be. See her body, her mind, her soul, the totality of her being, receive this priceless blessing.

'Good. Her heart is smiling now. The little girl's heart inside of you is also smiling now. She can love. She has found the place to conduct her hopes and dreams. It is indeed the best place that she could ever have dreamed of. It is a place where no amount of money can purchase, any amount of logic, and reason can now approach. Your heart, your wonderful loving heart is healed, never to be alone again…'

Sarah went out a happy lady and returned for her next and

last appointment, even happier.

'You'll never guess what happened when I got home after last week's session,' she gushed. 'By the time I got home, it was time to prepare dinner, which is pretty much what I do every weekday evening. I was in the kitchen peeling potatoes when I heard the front door open quietly and shut quietly. Straightaway I know my son has returned from school. Even the way the two of them come in through the door is markedly different. Where he does it nicely, she crashes and bashes as if to say, I'm here, get your gloves on. So there I am, waiting for my son to come to say hello like he normally does, but suddenly I feel a pair of loving, warm arms surround my waist and the sweet voice of a young girl, a voice I swear at first I didn't recognize says, 'Hi, Mum, I love you'. Can you believe it? I have never had such a loving exchange with her; with anyone before. It's a miracle and I want to thank you from the bottom of my heart. Who would've thought that just one hour before this happened, we were sending her so much love and within an hour, it had returned to me with interest?'

'Who'd have thought, eh?'

Love is like that. Hate is like that. Life is like that.

I believe that one must accept their 'quota' in life and not expect more. The rags and riches of this life have been predetermined by our desires and actions. I'm of the belief that we can't be a single penny richer or poorer than we are destined to be. But the heart can be enriched beyond our wildest dreams.

In my own topsy turvy life I already had everything I required to feel good about myself; successful, glamorous career, wonderful family, money, nice house. In the 80s and 90s I had so many incredible experiences that confirmed the vital need, at least in me, to ponder the imponderable questions, and seek true fulfilment.

Since my departure from the Rubettes in 1980 I only saw the group on the very odd occasion. One very odd occasion transpired at the Brentwood centre in Essex in the 1994 when 3000 fans of the 1970s piled into the theatre to get a rare glimpse of their ageing idols. As I remember it was a charity gig and I asked Alan if I could come and play a couple of numbers back on the drums just for the 'craic'. The gig was great and in the dressing rooms afterwards I thanked Alan for asking me to come and play. The drummer who had replaced me for many years, Alex, chipped in rather acerbically, 'He didn't actually. You did.'

Alex had moved behind me and started flipping back and forth my sikha, a knot of hair that Krishna devotees wear at the back of the head.

I decided enough was enough and spun round in a flash, jamming my up-raised knee a half inch from Alex's groin.

'All those years you've been a Krishna and you still can't control yourself,' he said, mockingly.

'Oh yes I can,' I replied. 'You're lucky Alex, fifteen years ago I'd have followed through.'

Boys will be boys, eh?

Eighteen

IN 2000 I MANAGED TO GET a new musical I had written on in the Haymarket Leicester, with the kind help of my friends Ian and Katrina Roberts. We had a limited budget for the production and so utilised the talents of a local acting school for the chorus line and four fully paid professionals for the main parts. The leading lady turned out to be a prima donna and so after a week of disturbed rehearsals we were forced to replace her. We chose an outstanding seventeen-year-old student, Parminder Kaur Nagara, as the leading lady and she proved an awesome replacement, wowing the audiences every night. I also had the gig as the orchestra's drummer and Scottie, my son, was the bassist

The Guardian wrote that it was a wonderful show and the only thing wrong with it was that there was not a CD to buy afterward so you could re-call Richardson's wonderful tunes. Parminder quickly went from this, her first professional show (albeit by default), to another professional engagement in London followed by the starring role in the movie, *Bend It Like Beckham*, and on to international acclaim in the long running American series ER.

There was one song from the musical that Boy George recorded with my daughter Pia (now known as Gaurangi) as a single to be taken from the show, called *Human Beings*. They sang it beautifully but at the last minute Virgin Records refused to give George a one-off contractual release. You can hear it on YouTube under *Human Beings*, Boy George and Gaurangi.

Alan from the Rubettes was the only person from my past who came to check out what I was up to, though many had said they'd try. Whenever someone says they'll try, you can be sure that they're never gonna come.

That same year, completely out of the blue, he turned up on my doorstep looking distinctly distressed. He was determined that I should return to the band after a twenty year absence. He had some rebellion in the ranks of the Rubettes and basically had been dropped in the proverbial by a couple of the band's members, including Alex. Incredibly, due to his Capricornian doggedness, he had kept the band going all those years, partly due to his tenacity, but mostly due to the fact that the prospect of a 'proper' job for him was as frightening as that trip over the Alps had been for me.

I was in the garden clinic with clients at the time of Alan's visit and so good old Cherrille dealt with the whole drama without my knowing that my whole life was about to change again.

Cherrille first said to Alan that she wasn't sure I would want to go back on the road after 20 long years away, but while they were on the subject, just how much was he prepared to pay me per gig?

Alan's first offer to lure my ageing bum back on the old drum stool, was laughingly dismissed by Cherrille, stating that I could earn that much in the back garden in a day's work. He satisfactorily upped his bid and when I came in, Cherrille, acting as my unelected manager, had the deal signed, sealed and delivered. I was back out on the road as part of the Old Grey Wrinkly Revolution.

We had been living our lives very simply with everything dedicated to the process of self realisation and I guess The

Upstairs Management wanted us to be able to afford to tend to our ailing house and its many needs with a bit of TLC. This new development meant we could begin long overdue refurbishments.

However, I was not sure that I could play drums any more. The last time I had appeared behind a drum-kit was for Boy George on his comeback record, *Bow Down Mister*. George had contacted Polystyrene from X-Ray Specks, who was also a Krishna devotee, to see if she could get some devotee singers to lay some backing vocals on a new album he was cutting at Olympic Studios, London around 1990.

We – me, Polly, Pia, (then called Gaurangi) and Laura Logic from X-Ray Specks sang alongside a London gospel choir and by comparison they outclassed us with their wonderful voices. However, at that time, I think I would not be dishonest to say we were living a very pure and renounced lifestyle and, as such, we gave it some welly, as they say in the trade, and we held our own. Tony, George's manager, and very much an avowed materialist, was visibly touched by our vocal offering and said he had been moved by the whole experience.

After reading George's palm (as you do), I told both Tony and George that he was coming back and of all the great tracks on the album, *Bow Down Mister* was the one that was going to do it. They appreciated what I had to say but I could sense that they had other ideas. Sure enough, they released another title which disappeared without a trace chart-wise. Then another, then another, then another, and finally *Bow Down Mister* and wham, Boy George was back and we appeared on all the big TV shows with him. That was literally the last time that I played. So how I was going to deal with this new life beckoning, the Lord only knew. Just while we're on the subject of George, I have to say that when he was 'clean' he was one of the sweetest persons you could know. Courteous, respectful of the devotees, very approachable and friendly to all. We lost contact as George got dragged back into the shadow world of intoxication.

He spent some difficult years in that space which eventually saw him incarcerated in prison for a year or so. I bumped into him in Denmark Street shortly after his release. I was amazed at how alive and free he was. Indeed he confirmed that prison had been the best thing that had happened for him in such a long time.

Through it he had to confront all his unresolved issues and even though he could have had all the drugs he dreamed of in that place, he chose to bravely face his stuff and live free from them and all that their sordid place in your life entails. He told me that for the first time in decades he had smelled the fragrance from the flowers in his back garden in Hampstead and it was such a deep and moving experience for him. Me too, just to see him so happy again.

Going back to the remnants of my distant past with my old group gave me not only the chance to earn a little more cash but the opportunity to meet some of my old mates from the 70s too; those who were alive, that is. Quite a few had succumbed to the attendant excesses of that lifestyle. It was interesting to see how I would deal with my old existence through my new life's eyes, and conversely, how it would view me. Pretty soon everyone on the stadium and concert hall tours in the UK and Europe knew that the madman was back and was now an austere Hare Krishna but they treated me and my lifestyle in the non-judgemental way that I treated their excesses.

After a few months I regained my stamina to be able to put on a half reasonable performance with the Rubes and in between, got on with seeing my private clients at home one day a week and going to the Soho Street temple every Tuesday to give class and afterward lead a band of chant-singing, cymbal-clashing, drum-bashing devotees up and down Oxford Street, which I still do today. We call it riding the Ox, as it feels like you are being carried on the back of something much stronger than you.

I got the opportunity to serve some of the other band members on these tours, doing regular massages on the hands and wrists of Romeo, Showaddywaddy's drummer, when they started to seize up. Another time in the middle of the Blitz Glitz Tour in 2003, Bruce, Sweet's brilliant drummer became very unwell and I was able to remember enough of my herbal remedy expertise to go out from the Holiday Inn and search in the surrounding countryside for the relevant herbs to sort him out. Everyone in the hotel breakfast room was howling with laughter as Bruce swigged the pungent concoction I had made him.

We did the Barnardos charity tour with Showaddywaddy, Alvin Stardust, Sweet and Mud and played all the big arenas in the UK.

Les from Mud, who was slowly destroying himself with booze, fell ill before the show in the Midlands and I invited myself into his dressing room where he lay, unable to move.

Les was also a diabetic but refused to have a doctor called in. I asked for the room to be cleared and got about doing my stuff on him. After one hour he was up and I was walking him up and down the corridors beneath the arena. He was able to perform. I begged him to lay off the booze but he was not hearing me. He said he'd had a good life and didn't give a toss what happened to him. A couple of years later, a massive heart attack took him out of the game forever.

A song of the lament over our intransigence and failure to recognise the great gift of this human life springs to mind:

Through past acts of merit and of worth
You were granted this human birth

And from day to day in age you gain
With each moment life does wane
When death comes nothing will stay
This precious chance might slip away
When once the leaf has broken free
It cannot then rejoin the tree.

It may be some time before dear Les can rejoin it, but rejoin it he eventually will. In the form of His Limitless Love, God's magic will reel him and all the rest of us reprobates back in. I remember at the end of Alvin Stardust's *This is Your Life* testimonial we, all the pop elite of the day were asked to move to the front of the stage with Alvin as he took the last applause and Jimmy Saville said, looking amongst our moteley crew 'God, if the devil cast his net he'd catch a few now'. He was right, many of us never made it through this far.

Dave Mount, Mud's drummer, met with a much more tragic end than even Les. He committed suicide around Christmas time, 2006. It was totally unexpected. As far as we knew his life seemed okay – maybe okay for some is not enough. The last time I saw him was at the Millennium Party at the BBC, Shepherd's Bush in 2000. He was working in insurance. I was quite taken aback as Dave had been a real live wire, with a wonderful sense of humour. When we made the film, Side By Side in 1976 with Barry Humphries and Terry Thomas, I got to know him quite well and he was full of life and fun. Insurance may have paid the bills but he was a drummer and comedian and perhaps he was dying inside. I don't know... What I do know is that Mickey Most, their record boss, gave them the absolute least royalties that any group have ever been paid, and whereas we, who were of a similar stature in terms of record success had nicely appointed big houses, they were all living in little flats.

It was great to hear that Mud's bass player eventually

joined the 60s group The Hollies and is doing well touring the world and that Rob Davis, Mud's talented guitarist, has become one of the top songwriters in Britain writing among many others the international best seller *I Can't Get You Out Of My Head* by Kylie Minogue.

Another artist who was also in Mickey Most's stable was Suzi Quatro. Fortunately, Suzi, being no pushover, fared somewhat better. There was an interesting occasion involving Suzi when we were gigging together around 2005 in Belgium. It took place in the Holiday Inn breakfast bar in Brussels.

I was talking to Romeo about reincarnation and Suzi, who was chatting with our concert promoter, Reiner, overheard our conversation and came over. Suzi is very much into paranormal things and is open minded about what folk have to say about spiritual subject matters.

Suzi told us that her departed mother was always with her and she often received guidance and direction from her. She also said that she was extremely attached to her mum and felt very dependent on her spiritual presence. Shortly after the conversation we left to get our luggage from our rooms to depart for the flight home.

As soon as I entered my room I had a strong sense of Suzi's mother. Thinking it was my imagination, as we had just been speaking about her, I dismissed the feeling. But very strongly and firmly I got the words, 'Please tell Suzi I'm happy that she's sorting her life nicely, but now I need to come back. There's more work that I have to do. Please tell her.'

With all the experiences I'd had, I still was not that confident about passing on messages like these, especially not to Suzi, who was so attached to her mum. I took the coward's way out and said nothing.

Several months later we were all playing together in a ten thousand seat concert hall in Dusseldorf. I was enjoying a moment of rare quiet before the performance. Unexpectedly,

Suzi found me and told me she had something amazing to tell me. I had a feeling I already knew, so told her about my vision before she had a chance to speak.

'I've known this for a couple of months, but due to its personal nature I didn't want to say in case you got hurt. Your mother came to me and told me that now you're finally getting yourself sorted she's decided to give up being your guide and return to work on herself. She's being re-born again.'

Suzi's face beamed with joy as she said, 'Thank you so much. I'll take that as confirmation of what happened to me.'

Suzi went on to explain how she was in the throes of finishing her last album. She tightened her grip on my hands.

'So I'm sitting in the studio waiting for the engineer to start the tape so I can put my vocals on, but the engineer begins talking to the assistant. You know me, normally I would get on their case for keeping me waiting. I'm looking at them and along the console behind the engineer's back a line of smoke appears,' she said, eerily.

'I'm thinking, Oh my God, there's a fire in the control room and they haven't even noticed it. But for some bizarre reason, I don't shout. It's so strange. I'm just sitting there, watching this smoky stuff slowly spiral up behind them and then ... I couldn't believe my eyes. My mother appeared in the smoke, as clear and concise as though she were really there. I was overcome with emotion and at the same time quietly calm and detached and... she said everything that you just told me.'

The account is related in Suzi's book, *Unzipped*, where she says my information came via a dream but it really came at the Holiday Inn, Brussels, via Supersoul.

Nineteen

THE MID 80S WAS A PERIOD when both my wife and daughter came with me each Saturday evening to chant in London. After a hard day's work in our health store in Romford we would go on the train to Soho Street temple to join the devotees in what is known as Maha Harinama – a large number of devotees chanting Krishna's names through the town or village of their choice, which in this case was the West End. We would then return to the Temple tired but full of sublime bliss.

Feeling particularly exhausted one Saturday I opted to stay in the temple room to chant alone, but someone told me I was needed for the Harinama.

The group of forty or so of us gathered outside the temple in Soho Street armed with clay drums, small hand cymbals, sanctified sweets to give out, and a bunch of sweet smelling incense to waft through the crowded streets.

We were dancing on air. It was a hot, humid night. Around 7.30 we arrived at the Eros statue in Piccadilly, which was surrounded by hundreds of Saturday night revellers intent on having a good time. It was so jam-packed, the procession slowed right down as we wended our musical way gently through the folk passing to and fro. Normally people are quite accepting of us, sometimes joining in or having their photographs taken alongside us. The police too are often quite favourable. Back in the early days, the first Harinama participants were instantly arrested and manhandled down to the Nick. One of our prominent Harinama leaders was the late great Tribhuvanath, a toothy, live-wired soul who sang and beat his love-filled heart out every day for years through London's busy streets as well as single-handedly heading up the Krishna festival programmes in many countries. One day when, for the umpteenth time he was dragged before the judge he had the foresight to bring some of our books explaining about Krishna Consciousness. The judge sensed that, regardless of his law breaking activities, he was in the presence of a formidably genuine man of God and thus read all the books Tribhuvanath had gifted.

The very next time he revisited the courtroom the judge threw the case out declaring heatedly to the police who had apprehended him that these people are actually doing our job for us, teaching folk a moral life through their literature. From that day the devotees have never had to have their saffron collars felt by the Bobbies. In fact, they seem to like us. They know apart from the spiritual ambience we create that we also bring a harmless sense of fun and joy to an often tensed and frightened city, but this humid summer's night was to prove somewhat of an exception.

I was about six pairs back from the front of the procession. My wife and daughter were somewhere toward the back. Then a big bruiser with a purple-coloured Mohican haircut ran out of the crowd seated around the steps of Eros, took a big swig of his Tennants, pushed his ugly mush within inches of one devotee and blasted the foaming contents of his even uglier mouth into his face.

The devotee just shook his head and peacefully pulled up the side of his robe to dry his face. His humility was impressive; he continued playing his cymbals and singing

The Mohican disappeared back into the crowd. There were

hundreds of people there so we couldn't move off quickly. But he soon reappeared, and flushed by his unopposed success, he came back for a repeat performance, with the same response. All I could think was that this devotee was so advanced in spiritual life to be able to tolerate such disrespect. I thought I must try to be like him, and our chanting continued, and just like before, the Mohican disappeared into the safety of the crowd.

Just when I thought it was all over and we were nearly free from the human grid-lock, that bloody pest of a Mohican tried again. This time he'd run out of beer to spit, so he started spitefully kicking our hero in size 12 Doc Martins.

Fuck being tolerant screamed the voice in my head (definitely not the Supersoul) and I sprung forward like a tiger and punched him with a right hand so hard he went down like a sack of potatoes. As he lay dazed on the ground I advised him as politely as I could not to get up or there'd be more where that came from.

His spiky haired tribe of hooligan braves began appearing from nowhere and everywhere .They were on the warpath.

I wasn't too spiritual at that moment: 'You bastards think you can attack devotees like they're nothing? Yeah? Come on! I'll show you who we are!'

I was worried, for beneath the bravado, my wrist was twisted from hitting his cheek bone and not his jaw. I knew it wouldn't hold out very long. But I needn't have worried. The cavalry was coming. Two devotees, Govinda Bhakta and Hari Kirtan, who were distributing books, just happened to be at the right place at the right time. They were both tough guys. Hari knew karate. He had recently dispatched (minus two front teeth) the leader of some anti-Krishna rugby supporters in Chinatown, and although Govinda was a big fellow, he was also expert in calming, cooling and schmoozing.

We were saved.

I couldn't see anything untoward and continued singing. I discovered later that after the Mohican's mates pulled my hapless victim back to his feet, they gave him a bottle which he tried to smash on the iron railings, and set about finding the devotee who'd floored him... me.

Damn I should've finished him when I had the chance.

Then Cherrille leapt into action, plucking the bottle from his nasty hand and giving him a right earful as well. Cherrille saved the day!

And a few devotees stayed chanting, blissfully unaware of the entire situation.

I can't say I condone violence. My excuse is that we are living in the age of Kali and this age is typified by quarrel and confusion. According to Vedic wisdom, Kali lasts for 432,000 years and we are just 5000 years into it.

One day I was travelling on the Central Line heading east to home in Hornchurch, still dressed in my devotional clothes. I often get strange looks.

I remembered 30 years previous pulling in to Stratford Station on my way to the recording studio as a newly successful Rubette. It was a Friday, the day the new music mags were on sale, and a girl sitting opposite was studying the front page of the Record Mirror, a popular teen read of the time.

Our picture was plastered all over it. After studying our picture adoringly and telling her mate she fancied the drummer, she looked up and saw her musical eye-candy sitting within a couple of feet. She didn't know whether to smile or swoon or ask for my autograph. I was lapping it up.

Now, thirty years later on the same train in the same station, I'm about to attract some unwanted attention that certainly didn't require an autograph.

Three youngsters, their eyes bleary from openly sniffing

glue, moved from one part of the carriage to occupy on the seats right opposite me.

One of them slid something behind his back to his mate. It's a hammer.

Hare Krishna Hare Krishna, I kept repeating quietly.

The one in the middle brought a mace can to the side of his leg and suddenly the world wasn't looking as rosy as it had a few minutes earlier.

Hare Krishna, Hare Krishna.

In my normal consciousness I would by this time have taken some evasive action, or perhaps even got to them before they got to me but because I was so blissed out by the chanting, I didn't panic. I wasn't resigned to the imminent beating either. I was in a detached space.

The middle one, whose lips were cracked and face spotty from so much glue sniffing, yells, 'What's that shit on your face?'

His mates seemed to perceive this as a sign of imminent attack as their hands tightened around their ammunition, their bodies straightening in their seats.

'It's Tilak,' I laconically replied.

'What the fuck is Tilak?'

'It's clay from a sacred place in India that the Hare Krishna devotees place on their body.'

'What, before they die?' interrupted one of them, threateningly.

The one with the mace swiftly thrust the can right in front of my eyes. I didn't react.

'No, we wear it when we go out chanting on the streets.'

'Arry Arry Arry Arry Arry!' they began to chant.

'That's right,' I said, with the mace and my nose cosying up to one another like old buddies.

'You know Boy George's song *Bow Down Mister*?'

They all burst into Arry Arry Arry Krishna.

'Well I played drums and sang on it.'

'Sure ya fuckin' did!' They began pissing themselves with laughter.

At Stratford they just disappeared into the busy rush hour crowds, laughing their inebriated heads off.

In close proximity to Stratford station were the TV studios for *Big Breakfast*, a popular morning programme in the 90s. One week the main celebrity guest was the boxer Frank Bruno. He had just become the new heayweight champion of the world by defeating the American Oliver McCall. I had some short time previously got to know Frank through my work as a therapist. He had been recommended to me by a former client of mine. Frank was feeling, so to speak, at a loose end since his defeat at the hands of the brilliant Lennox Lewis. Boxing pundits had unanimously agreed that he should hang up his gloves and call it a day. Even the boxing commentator Harry Carpenter, a great friend of Frank's, had agreed with them. Carpenter had interviewed him after every major fight and Frank and Harry's post-fight televised *tete a tete*s had become as popular as the fighter himself. From these frequent interchanges a catchphrase inadvertently sprang forth: 'Yer know what I mean 'Arry?' More about that later.

I set about trying to help Frank, through hypnosis and counselling, to reignite his career. The way I approached the issue was to clear out all the mental and emotional rubbish from his difficult early years and then 'future pace' him to the time when he will become world champ, then take him backward through the fight experience to see how he did it. Then simply 'anchor' all that positive data within the subconscious mind.

After six treatments we seemed to be getting on really well together and his spirits had lifted. Then suddenly his wife Laura appeared and took me into a side room of their palatial home in Ongar. She got straight to the point.

'I know you've got enough on Frank to go to the newspapers. He's told you all about his life'.

I could see where this was going so I interrupted.

'You don't have to worry I have come to give you something not to take anything from you... Just chill!'

That was the last time I saw or heard from Frank save that is for our fortuitous meeting at Big Breakfast studios in Stratford after the 'miracle' of his win over McCall.

A dozen Krishna devotees (which included myself) had received a surprise call from the TV show to appear just before dawn at their Stratford centre.

We were thrilled. We were going to be allowed to chant the Hare Krishna mantra on nationwide TV. Yippee!!

We were first of all asked to stand in a line by a red bus while Blakey and Frank did a skit, then Frank came past.

'Nice fancy dress lads.'

'This is the real thing Frank,' I replied.

'Do I know you?' Frank said, looking at me closely.

'It's me, John!'

Frank stepped forward and shook my hand.

'How are yer, mate?'

I don't know if he recognised me but I chirpily replied, 'Fine!'

Later in the show they told us it was our chance to chant. We couldn't believe it. They were going to let us do our thing We took up our drums and cymbals and danced and sang in the yard outside the house.

Then I realised why we had been booked for the show, for as we moved along around the cobbled courtyard Frank had quickly donned a devotee shirt and hand cymbals and was singing, 'Harry Carpenter! Harry Carpenter! Arry Arry! Arry Arry! Yer know what I mean Arry.'

We took it all in good spirits and at the show's end I (being the opportunist I am) called out to Frank.

'We have a special gift for you, Frank.'

It was near Christmas time, so I started singing some spontaneous words to the tune of We Wish You a Merry Christmas.

'We wish you a Hare Krishna. We wish you a Hare Krishna We wish you a Hare Krishna and a Hare New Year. Good tidings we bring, since you became King...'

As the titles for the shows end came up we erupted into the Hare Krishna mantra, jumping and bouncing in ecstacy.

Dressing and acting so conspicuously brings amazing variegated responses. The folk are like the weather, you never quite know what's gonna come next. English weather can be so fickle that you can experience four seasons in one day.

I have been taught that Universal weather passes through four seasons just as the Earth does. The universal turning of the seasons is much longer than twelve months of our earthly time; the Spring Season lasts 1,728,000 years; Summer 1,296,000 years, Autumn 864,000 years and Winter lasts for 432,000 years. These seasons are known respectively as the Golden (*Satya*), Silver (*Treta*), Bronze (*Dwarpara*) and Iron (*Kali*) ages.

Satya begins the cycle and houses living entities who are well-behaved, in the mode of goodness, yoga-loving, peaceful individuals. The process for these folk to return home to the spiritual world, if they should desire to do so, is *astanga* yoga, but it is a very exacting process and requires thousands of years of training to perfect it. Fortunately, the body that a *Satya* individual uses has a 'shelf life' of around 100,000 years, so Satyas have time to perfect.

After *Satya*, Yuga passes on to *Treta Yuga*, and the age span decreases to 10,000 years. The *astanga* yoga process for self-realisation is no longer appropriate for Tretas, as it takes around 60,000 years to perfect and they only live for 10,000. So, the Upstairs Management, always being desirous for our deliverance from our worldy prison house, recommend the lengthy but manageable system of sacrifice, which entails chanting of mantras and offering into the flame of sacrifice massive amounts of ghee, sandalwood and expensive oils plus other sacrificial paraphernalia fashioned from gold and precious materials along with sacred mantras as indicated by the Vedas.

At the next juncture, *Dwarpara*, the 10,000 year life span is again reduced to 1,000 years. The opulence that was still readily available in Treta Yuga is now not as easily accessed, as the Earth, incrementally, withdraws her resources back into herself. The consciousness of humanity is also dwindling and along with that there is a lessening of morals, good fortune and facility.

The process recommended by the Vedas during *Dwarpara* is deity worship, which although requiring a substantial amount of opulence, is nowhere near the amount required to perform sacrifice as in the previous yuga. This *Dwarpara Yuga* finished around 5,000 years ago, about the time the Old Testament and the Vedas were said to be written.

We observe that the ages of Old Testament prophets such as Methusalah, Noah and others were around the 800 year mark so we can deduce that they may have been living in the time of *Dwarapa Yuga*. Christians themselves very often question the veracity of the statements regarding their Old Testament prophets ages but we can see that they correspond to the Vedic version.

Finally, we enter into the winter period, *Kali Yuga*, where we are at present. This is the most difficult age to be incarnated, for as I have already said, it is typified by quarrel and hypocrisy. It is the age of war. So what then is the process for this age, where it is predicted that eventually the average life span will be around 20–25?

All rivers dry up. No fruit grows, only brambles and thorns, and men and women will run to the hills from the demoniac rulers, seek shelter in caves, and subsist on roots and leaves.

The Kali Yuga is typified by a preponderance of focus on the body's comforts and joys as we become more and more obsessed with its unending desire for satisfaction, at any cost. We will beg, steal, borrow, maim and kill to preserve our right to have this comfort, and woe betide anyone who tries to take it from us.

Lifespan at the beginning of Kali, like in the other ages, is reduced to one tenth, taking us down to 100 years, and the yoga – the sacrifices and the opulent deity worship of bygone ages – is no longer possible. The Vedic literature written from the all-knowing heart of Veda Vyasa, millennia ago, foresaw our worsening plight and gave us a process which all can take part in without fear of disqualification:

Hare nama, hare nama, hare nama eva kevalam
Kalau nastyeva, nastyeva, nastyeva, gatir anyatha

'In this age of quarrel and hypocrisy, the way to get free from Kali's coils is to chant the names of God.'

This chanting of the names of God is recommended in many of the world's major religions. The Old Testament advises, 'Thou shalt chant the Name of thy Lord with cymbal and drum'.

Allah, Buddha, Jehovah, Rama, God – All are Krishna, All are One.

Krishna says in the *Bhagavad Gita* that however a person surrenders to Him, it doesn't change the fact that He rewards them appropriately and accordingly. He also says for those of differing faiths that we should not disturb them.

When Krishna devotees chant we are calling out to every manifestation of Godhead, but specifically to Him in His wonderful form as an eternally adolescent youth with blooming eyes like lotus petals and a soft silken skin tinged with the hue of blue clouds.

I honestly believe that knowledge of the reincarnation process, and the Laws of Karma that inextricably attend it, are the key principles that will bring one and all to the same party, speaking the same language. It is a vital prerequisite towards creating the framework by which we can establish the blueprint for, at worst, tolerance and, at best, Love.

The Laws of Karma are as intractable and inescapable as the Good Lord who set them up. And if we listen to his party plans, we are going to be dancing in ecstasy before we know it. He is the ultimate enjoyer. Since the beginning of our earthly time we have challenged his right by vainly attempting to have our own personal pleasures without him and all the divine pleasures he wants to bestow upon us.

How to know if any of this bears the slightest semblance to truth? Experiment with it. And how does a scientist experiment? Partially or impartially?

Partial experimentation is no experimentation at all, so if you are ready, please read the wisdoms of the *Bhagavad Gita* and the ancient Vedic texts, and discover for yourself how much each of us have in common with one another, regardless of religious persuasion.

I feel amazingly honoured to have been privy to all this first hand information about the transmigration of the soul. I am not the kind of person who could have easily accepted controversial spiritual or supernatural statements without some kind of proof. But proof has been presented to me over and over again: the lady who was a horse, the demigod on the Sun,

Mozart living in America... These are just a few of thousands of stories that I could present to show that there is something massive is going on.

Each of life's debatable experiences is attended by so many cons: controversy, conspiracy, contention. Whether or not these revelations are the product of an over-developed sense of grandiosity on my part, it has left me with a sense of awe and respect for the mechanism of existence which is known by many names, but which I call God, or Krishna.

I have come to another con: a conclusion. Whoever or whatever is behind all this, it is palpably clear to me that we are living right slap bang inside the biggest conspiracy theory that ever existed! I sense it is the Conspiracy of Love. Although these stories cannot be cited as axiomatic proof of other worldly realities, they have at least jolted me from my materialistic somnambulism.

I am not expecting everyone to believe some of the accounts in my story, but by thinking about them, it may be that you will find something in them that makes you question and seek. And if you are already questioning and seeking they may lead you on toward the ultimate state as finder.

Love,

John (Jayadev) Richardson

To get news of John's work visit:

yoga.supersoul.com
mantrachoir.com

For details of John's recordings contact
New World Music at:

newworldmusic.com

Rubettes sites:

www.rubettes.com
www.rubettesfeaturingalanwilliams.com

Index